Boost.Asio C++ Network Programming Cookbook

Over 25 hands-on recipes to create robust and highly-efficient cross-platform distributed applications with the Boost.Asio library

Dmytro Radchuk

[PACKT] open source*
PUBLISHING   community experience distilled

BIRMINGHAM - MUMBAI

Boost.Asio C++ Network Programming Cookbook

First published: January 2016

Production reference: 1190116

Published by Packt Publishing Ltd.
Livery Place
35 Livery Street
Birmingham B3 2PB, UK.

ISBN 978-1-78398-654-5

www.packtpub.com

Credits

Author
Dmytro Radchuk

Reviewer
Victor Sigler

Commissioning Editor
Usha Iyer

Acquisition Editors
Shaon Basu

Manish Nainani

Content Development Editor
Samantha Gonsalves

Technical Editor
Madhunikita Sunil Chindarkar

Copy Editors
Trishya Hazare

Rashmi Sawant

Project Coordinator
Kinjal Bari

Proofreader
Safis Editing

Indexer
Hemangini Bari

Production Coordinator
Shantanu N. Zagade

Cover Work
Shantanu N. Zagade

About the Author

Dmytro Radchuk is a software engineer from Kyiv, Ukraine. His passion for science started at a young age and led him to receive a degree in computer science from Kyiv Polytechnic University. As of today, he has deep technical knowledge and more than 8 years of experience in the field of software development for several industries and businesses. He strongly believes that the whole is greater than the sum of its parts and this is one of the reasons why the development of distributed applications has become his main specialization.

Dmytro has always supported the idea of sharing knowledge and this has resulted in *Boost. Asio C++ Network Programming Cookbook*, which has become his first officially published book. He believes that science will help us deal with the monotony of everyday life. When he is not exploring another facet of computer engineering, he is probably learning a new aspect of psychology, history, or the arts, which are also of great interest to him.

I would like to dedicate this book to my fiancée, Anelia, for all her love and support.

About the Reviewer

Victor Sigler is an iOS software engineer with experience in developing consumer and enterprise mobile applications. He loves everything that is related to Apple and is passionate about Swift and the world of programming contests, where he has spent a long time developing in C++. He enjoys writing about iOS development in his blog at `http://www. vsigler.com` and also enjoys helping people with their queries on Stack Overflow. He can be found on Twitter as `@Vkt0r`. He has worked as a technical reviewer for *Swift 2 Design Patterns*, Packt Publishing.

www.PacktPub.com

Support files, eBooks, discount offers, and more

For support files and downloads related to your book, please visit www.PacktPub.com.

Did you know that Packt offers eBook versions of every book published, with PDF and ePub files available? You can upgrade to the eBook version at www.PacktPub.com and as a print book customer, you are entitled to a discount on the eBook copy. Get in touch with us at service@packtpub.com for more details.

At www.PacktPub.com, you can also read a collection of free technical articles, sign up for a range of free newsletters and receive exclusive discounts and offers on Packt books and eBooks.

https://www2.packtpub.com/books/subscription/packtlib

Do you need instant solutions to your IT questions? PacktLib is Packt's online digital book library. Here, you can search, access, and read Packt's entire library of books.

Why subscribe?

- ► Fully searchable across every book published by Packt
- ► Copy and paste, print, and bookmark content
- ► On demand and accessible via a web browser

Free access for Packt account holders

If you have an account with Packt at www.PacktPub.com, you can use this to access PacktLib today and view 9 entirely free books. Simply use your login credentials for immediate access.

Table of Contents

Preface

In today's information-centric globalized world, telecommunications have become an essential part of our lives. They penetrate and play crucial roles in almost every aspect of our day-to-day activities, from personal to professional. Sometimes, a failure to communicate information correctly and on time may lead to significant loss of material assets or even casualties.

Therefore, it is very important to provide the highest level of reliability when it comes to developing telecommunication software. However, it can be a really challenging task due to the inherent complexity of the domain and accidental complexity of the low-level tools provided by modern operating systems.

The Boost.Asio library is aimed at reducing accidental complexity by introducing type systems and exploiting object-oriented methods, and decreasing the development time by providing high degrees of reusability. In addition to this, because the library is cross-platform, the applications implemented with it can be built on multiple platforms, which enhances software qualities even more, while decreasing its costs.

This book contains more than 30 recipes—step-by-step solutions to various tasks that often (and not so often) arise in the area of network programming. All recipes take advantage of facilities provided by the Boost.Asio library, demonstrating best practices of applying the library to execute typical tasks and solve different problems.

What this book covers

Chapter 1, *The Basics*, introduces you to basic classes provided by the Boost.Asio library and demonstrates how to execute basic operations, such as resolving a DNS name, connecting a socket, accepting a connection, and so on.

Chapter 2, *I/O Operations*, demonstrates how to perform individual network I/O operations, both synchronous and asynchronous.

Chapter 3, *Implementing Client Applications*, contains recipes that demonstrate how to implement different types of client applications.

Chapter 4, *Implementing Server Applications*, contains recipes that demonstrate how to implement different types of server applications.

Chapter 5, *HTTP and SSL/TLS*, covers more advanced topics on the HTTP and SSL/TLS protocol implementation.

Chapter 6, *Other Topics*, includes recipes that discuss less popular but still quite important topics, such as timers, socket options, composite buffers, and others.

What you need for this book

To compile samples presented in this book, you will need Visual Studio 2012+ on Windows or GCC 4.7+ on Unix platforms.

Who this book is for

If you want to enhance your C++ network programming skills using the Boost.Asio library and understand the theory behind the development of distributed applications, this book is just what you need. The prerequisite for this book is to have a basic knowledge of C++11. To get the most from the book and comprehend advanced topics, you will need some background experience in multithreading.

Sections

In this book, you will find several headings that appear frequently (Getting ready, How to do it, How it works, There's more, and See also).

To give clear instructions on how to complete a recipe, we use these sections as follows:

Getting ready

This section tells you what to expect in the recipe, and describes how to set up any software or any preliminary settings required for the recipe.

How to do it...

This section contains the steps required to follow the recipe.

How it works...

This section usually consists of a detailed explanation of what happened in the previous section.

There's more...

This section consists of additional information about the recipe in order to make the reader more knowledgeable about the recipe.

See also

This section provides helpful links to other useful information for the recipe.

Conventions

In this book, you will find a number of text styles that distinguish between different kinds of information. Here are some examples of these styles and an explanation of their meaning.

Code words in text, database table names, folder names, filenames, file extensions, pathnames, dummy URLs, user input, and Twitter handles are shown as follows: "In Boost.Asio a passive socket is represented by the `asio::ip::tcp::acceptor` class."

A block of code is set as follows:

```
std::shared_ptr<boost::asio::ip::tcp::socket> m_sock;
boost::asio::streambuf m_request;
std::map<std::string, std::string> m_request_headers;
std::string m_requested_resource;
```

When we wish to draw your attention to a particular part of a code block, the relevant lines or items are set in bold:

```
std::shared_ptr<boost::asio::ip::tcp::socket> m_sock;
boost::asio::streambuf m_request;
std::map<std::string, std::string> m_request_headers;
std::string m_requested_resource;
```

New terms and **important words** are shown in bold.

Warnings or important notes appear in a box like this.

Tips and tricks appear like this.

Reader feedback

Feedback from our readers is always welcome. Let us know what you think about this book—what you liked or disliked. Reader feedback is important for us as it helps us develop titles that you will really get the most out of.

To send us general feedback, simply e-mail feedback@packtpub.com, and mention the book's title in the subject of your message.

If there is a topic that you have expertise in and you are interested in either writing or contributing to a book, see our author guide at www.packtpub.com/authors.

Customer support

Now that you are the proud owner of a Packt book, we have a number of things to help you to get the most from your purchase.

Downloading the example code

You can download the example code files from your account at http://www.packtpub.com for all the Packt Publishing books you have purchased. If you purchased this book elsewhere, you can visit http://www.packtpub.com/support and register to have the files e-mailed directly to you.

Errata

Although we have taken every care to ensure the accuracy of our content, mistakes do happen. If you find a mistake in one of our books—maybe a mistake in the text or the code—we would be grateful if you could report this to us. By doing so, you can save other readers from frustration and help us improve subsequent versions of this book. If you find any errata, please report them by visiting http://www.packtpub.com/submit-errata, selecting your book, clicking on the **Errata Submission Form** link, and entering the details of your errata. Once your errata are verified, your submission will be accepted and the errata will be uploaded to our website or added to any list of existing errata under the Errata section of that title.

To view the previously submitted errata, go to https://www.packtpub.com/books/content/support and enter the name of the book in the search field. The required information will appear under the **Errata** section.

Piracy

Piracy of copyrighted material on the Internet is an ongoing problem across all media. At Packt, we take the protection of our copyright and licenses very seriously. If you come across any illegal copies of our works in any form on the Internet, please provide us with the location address or website name immediately so that we can pursue a remedy.

Please contact us at copyright@packtpub.com with a link to the suspected pirated material.

We appreciate your help in protecting our authors and our ability to bring you valuable content.

Questions

If you have a problem with any aspect of this book, you can contact us at questions@packtpub.com, and we will do our best to address the problem.

1

The Basics

In this chapter, we will cover:

- ▶ Creating an endpoint
- ▶ Creating an active socket
- ▶ Creating a passive socket
- ▶ Resolving a DNS name
- ▶ Binding a socket to an endpoint
- ▶ Connecting a socket
- ▶ Accepting connections

Introduction

Computer networks and communication protocols significantly increase capabilities of modern software, allowing different applications or separate parts of the same application to communicate with each other to achieve a common goal. Some applications have communication as their main function, for example, instant messengers, e-mail servers and clients, file download software, and so on. Others have the network communication layer as a fundamental component, on top of which the main functionality is built. Some of the examples of such applications are web browsers, network file systems, distributed database management systems, media streaming software, online games, offline games with multiplayer over the network option support, and many others. Besides, nowadays almost any application in addition to its main functionality provides supplementary functions, involving network communication. The most prominent examples of such functions are online registration and automatic software update. In the latter case, the update package is downloaded from the application developer's remote server and installed on the user's computer or mobile device.

The application that consists of two or more parts, each of which runs on a separate computing device, and communicates with other parts over a computer network is called a **distributed application**. For example, a web server and a web browser together can be considered as one complex distributed application. The browser running on a user's computer communicates with the web server running on a different remote computer in order to achieve a common goal—to transmit and display a web page requested by the user.

Distributed applications provide significant benefits as compared to traditional applications running on a single computer. The most valuable of them are the following:

- ▶ Ability to transmit data between two or more remote computing devices. This is absolutely obvious and the most valuable benefit of distributed software.

- ▶ Ability to connect computers in a network and install special software on them, creating powerful computing systems that can perform tasks that can't otherwise be performed on a single computer in an adequate amount of time.

- ▶ Ability to effectively store and share data in a network. In a computer network, a single device can be used as data storage to store big amounts of data and other devices can easily request some portions of that data when necessary without the need to keep the copy of all data on each device. As an example, consider large datacenters hosting hundreds of millions of websites. The end user can request the web page they need anytime by sending the request to the server over the network (usually, the Internet). There is no need to keep the copy of the website on the user's device. There is a single storage of the data (a website) and millions of users can request the data from that storage if and when this information is needed.

For two applications running on different computing devices to communicate with each other, they need to agree on a communication protocol. Of course, the developer of the distributed application is free to implement his or her own protocol. However, this would be rarely the case at least for two reasons. First, developing such a protocol is an enormously complex and time-consuming task. Secondly, such protocols are already defined, standardized, and even implemented in all popular operating systems including Windows, Mac OS X, and majority of the distributions of Linux.

These protocols are defined by the TCP/IP standard. Don't be fooled by the standard's name; it defines not only TCP and IP but many more other protocols, comprising a TCP/IP protocol stack with one or more protocols on each level of the stack. Distributed software developers usually deal with transport level protocols such as TCP or UDP. Lower layer protocols are usually hidden from the developer and are handled by the operating system and network devices.

In this book, we only touch upon TCP and UDP protocols that satisfy the needs of most developers of distributed software. If the reader is not familiar with the TCP/IP protocol stack, the OSI model, or TCP and UDP protocols, it's highly advised to read some theory on these topics. Though this book provides some brief information about them, it is mostly focused on practical aspects of using TCP and UDP protocols in distributed software development.

The TCP protocol is a transport layer protocol with the following characteristics:

- It's reliable, which means that this protocol guarantees delivery of the messages in proper order or a notification that the message has not been delivered. The protocol includes error handling mechanisms, which frees the developer from the need to implement them in the application.

- It assumes logical connection establishment. Before one application can communicate with another over the TCP protocol, it must establish a logical connection by exchanging service messages according to the standard.

- It assumes the point-to-point communication model. That is, only two applications can communicate over a single connection. No multicast messaging is supported.

- It is stream-oriented. This means that the data being sent by one application to another is interpreted by the protocol as a stream of bytes. In practice, it means that if a sender application sends a particular block of data, there is no guarantee that it will be delivered to the receiver application as the same block of data in a single turn, that is, the sent message may be broken into as many parts as the protocol _wants_ and each of them will be delivered separately, though in correct order.

The UDP protocol is a transport layer protocol having different (in some sense opposite) characteristics from those of the TCP protocol. The following are its characteristics:

- It's unreliable, which means that if a sender sends a message over a UDP protocol, there is no guarantee that the message will be delivered. The protocol won't try to detect or fix any errors. The developer is responsible for all error handling.

- It's connectionless, meaning that no connection establishment is needed before the applications can communicate.

- It supports both one-to-one and one-to-many communication models. Multicast messages are supported by the protocol.

- It's datagram oriented. This means that the protocol interprets data as messages of a particular size and will try to deliver them as a whole. The message (datagram) either will be delivered as a whole, or if the protocol fails to do that won't be delivered at all.

Because the UDP protocol is unreliable, it is usually used in reliable local networks. To use it for communication over the Internet (which is an unreliable network), the developer must implement error handling mechanisms in its application.

When there is a need to communicate over the Internet, the TCP protocol is most often the best choice due to its reliability.

As it has already been mentioned, both TCP and UDP protocols and the underlying protocols required by them are implemented by most popular operating systems. A developer of a distributed application is provided an API through which it can use protocols implementation. The TCP/IP standard does not standardize the protocol API implementation; therefore, several API implementations exist. However, the one based on **Berkeley Sockets API** is the most widely used.

Berkeley Sockets API is the name of one of the many possible implementations of TCP and UDP protocols' API. This API was developed at the Berkeley University of California, USA (hence the name) in the early 1980s. It is built around a concept of an abstract object called a **socket**. Such a name was given to this object in order to draw the analogy with a usual electrical socket. However, this idea seems to have somewhat failed due to the fact that Berkeley Sockets turned out to be a significantly more complex concept.

Now Windows, Mac OS X, and Linux operating systems all have this API implemented (though with some minor variations) and software developers can use it to consume TCP and UDP protocols' functionality when developing distributed applications.

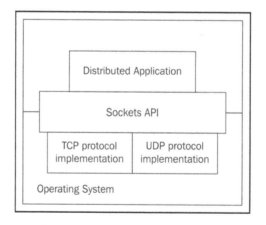

Though very popular and widely used, Sockets API has several flaws. First, because it was designed as a very generic API that should support many different protocols, it is quite complex and somewhat difficult to use. The second flaw is that this is a C-style functional API with a poor type system, which makes it error prone and even more difficult to use. For example, Sockets API doesn't provide a separate type representing a socket. Instead, the built-in type `int` is used, which means that by mistake any value of the `int` type can be passed as an argument to the function expecting a socket, and the compiler won't detect the mistake. This may lead to run-time crashes, the root cause of which is hard to find.

Network programming is inherently complex and doing it with a low-level C-style socket API makes it even more complex and error prone. Boost.Asio is an O-O C++ library that is, just like raw Sockets API, built around the concept of a *socket*. Roughly speaking, Boost.Asio wraps raw Sockets API and provides the developer with O-O interface to it. It is intended to simplify network programming in several ways as follows:

- It hides the raw C-style API and providing a user with an object-oriented API

- It provides a rich-type system, which makes code more readable and allows it to catch many errors at compilation time

- As Boost.Asio is a cross-platform library, it simplifies development of cross-platform distributed applications

- It provides auxiliary functionality such as scatter-gather I/O operations, stream-based I/O, exception-based error handling, and others

- The library is designed so that it can be relatively easily extended to add new custom functionality

This chapter introduces essential Boost.Asio classes and demonstrates how to perform basic operations with them.

Creating an endpoint

A typical client application, before it can communicate with a server application to consume its services, must obtain the IP address of the host on which the server application is running and the protocol port number associated with it. A pair of values consisting of an IP address and a protocol port number that uniquely identifies a particular application running on a particular host in a computer network is called an **endpoint**.

The client application will usually obtain the IP address and the port number identifying the server application either from the user directly through the application UI or as command-line arguments or will read it from the application's configuration file.

The IP address can be represented as a string containing an address in dot-decimal notation if it is an IPv4 address (for example, `192.168.10.112`) or in hexadecimal notation if it is an IPv6 address (for example, `FE36::0404:C3FA:EF1E:3829`). Besides, the server IP address can be provided to the client application in an indirect form, as a string containing a DNS name (for example, `localhost` or `www.google.com`). Another way to represent an IP address is an integer value. The IPv4 address is represented as a 32-bit integer and IPv6 as a 64-bit integer. However, due to poor readability and memorability this representation is used extremely rarely.

If the client application is provided with a DNS name before it can communicate with the server application, it must resolve the DNS name to obtain the actual IP address of the host running the server application. Sometimes, the DNS name may map to multiple IP addresses, in which case the client may want to try addresses one by one until it finds the one that works. We'll consider a recipe describing how to resolve DNS names with Boost.Asio later in this chapter.

The server application needs to deal with endpoints too. It uses the endpoint to specify to the operating system on which the IP address and protocol port it wants to listen for incoming messages from the clients. If the host running the server application has only one network interface and a single IP address assigned to it, the server application has only one option as to on which address to listen. However, sometimes the host might have more than one network interface and correspondingly more than one IP address. In this situation, the server application encounters a difficult problem of selecting an appropriate IP address on which to listen for incoming messages. The problem is that the application knows nothing about details such as underlying IP protocol settings, packet routing rules, DNS names which are mapped to the corresponding IP addresses, and so on. Therefore, it is quite a complex task (and sometimes even not solvable) for the server application to foresee through which IP address the messages sent by clients will be delivered to the host.

If the server application chooses only one IP address to listen for incoming messages, it may miss messages routed to other IP addresses of the host. Therefore, the server application usually wants to listen on all IP addresses available on the host. This guarantees that the server application will receive all messages arriving at any IP address and the particular protocol port.

To sum up, the endpoints serve two goals:

 ▶ The client application uses an endpoint to designate a particular server application it wants to communicate with.
 ▶ The server application uses an endpoint to specify a local IP address and a port number on which it wants to receive incoming messages from clients. If there is more than one IP address on the host, the server application will want to create a special endpoint representing all IP addresses at once.

This recipe explains how to create endpoints in Boost.Asio both in client and server applications.

Getting ready

Before creating the endpoint, the client application must obtain the raw IP address and the protocol port number designating the server it will communicate with. The server application on the other hand, as it usually listens for incoming messages on all IP addresses, only needs to obtain a port number on which to listen.

Here, we don't consider how the application obtains a raw IP address or a port number. In the following recipes, we assume that the IP address and the port number have already been obtained by the application and are available at the beginning of the corresponding algorithm.

How to do it...

The following algorithms and corresponding code samples demonstrate two common scenarios of creating an endpoint. The first one demonstrates how the client application can create an endpoint to specify the server it wants to communicate with. The second one demonstrates how the server application creates an endpoint to specify on which IP addresses and port it wants to listen for incoming messages from clients.

Creating an endpoint in the client to designate the server

The following algorithm describes steps required to perform in the client application to create an endpoint designating a server application the client wants to communicate with. Initially, the IP address is represented as a string in the dot-decimal notation if this is an IPv4 address or in hexadecimal notation if this is an IPv6 address:

1. Obtain the server application's IP address and port number. The IP address should be specified as a string in the dot-decimal (IPv4) or hexadecimal (IPv6) notation.

2. Represent the raw IP address as an object of the `asio::ip::address` class.

3. Instantiate the object of the `asio::ip::tcp::endpoint` class from the address object created in step 2 and a port number.

4. The endpoint is ready to be used to designate the server application in Boost.Asio communication related methods.

The following code sample demonstrates possible implementation of the algorithm:

```
#include <boost/asio.hpp>
#include <iostream>

using namespace boost;

int main()
{
  // Step 1. Assume that the client application has already
  // obtained the IP-address and the protocol port number.
  std::string raw_ip_address = "127.0.0.1";
  unsigned short port_num = 3333;

  // Used to store information about error that happens
  // while parsing the raw IP-address.
  boost::system::error_code ec;
```

```
// Step 2. Using IP protocol version independent address
// representation.
asio::ip::address ip_address =
  asio::ip::address::from_string(raw_ip_address, ec);

if (ec.value() != 0) {
  // Provided IP address is invalid. Breaking execution.
  std::cout
    << "Failed to parse the IP address. Error code = "
    << ec.value() << ". Message: " << ec.message();
    return ec.value();
}

// Step 3.
asio::ip::tcp::endpoint ep(ip_address, port_num);

// Step 4. The endpoint is ready and can be used to specify a
// particular server in the network the client wants to
// communicate with.

return 0;
}
```

Creating the server endpoint

The following algorithm describes steps required to perform in a server application to create an endpoint specifying all IP addresses available on the host and a port number on which the server application wants to listen for incoming messages from the clients:

1. Obtain the protocol port number on which the server will listen for incoming requests.
2. Create a special instance of the `asio::ip::address` object representing all IP addresses available on the host running the server.
3. Instantiate an object of the `asio::ip::tcp::endpoint` class from the address object created in step 2 and a port number.
4. The endpoint is ready to be used to specify to the operating system that the server wants to listen for incoming messages on all IP addresses and a particular protocol port number.

The following code sample demonstrates possible implementation of the algorithm. Note that it is assumed that the server application is going to communicate over the IPv6 protocol:

```
#include <boost/asio.hpp>
#include <iostream>
```

```
using namespace boost;

int main()
{
  // Step 1. Here we assume that the server application has
  //already obtained the protocol port number.
  unsigned short port_num = 3333;

  // Step 2. Create special object of asio::ip::address class
  // that specifies all IP-addresses available on the host. Note
  // that here we assume that server works over IPv6 protocol.
  asio::ip::address ip_address = asio::ip::address_v6::any();

  // Step 3.
  asio::ip::tcp::endpoint ep(ip_address, port_num);

  // Step 4. The endpoint is created and can be used to
  // specify the IP addresses and a port number on which
  // the server application wants to listen for incoming
  // connections.

  return 0;
}
```

How it works...

Let's consider the first code sample. The algorithm it implements is applicable in an application playing a role of a client that is an application that actively initiates the communication session with a server. The client application needs to be provided an IP address and a protocol port number of the server. Here we assume that those values have already been obtained and are available at the beginning of the algorithm, which makes step 1 details a given.

Having obtained the raw IP address, the client application must represent it in terms of the Boost.Asio type system. Boost.Asio provides three classes used to represent an IP address:

- ▶ `asio::ip::address_v4`: This represents an IPv4 address
- ▶ `asio::ip::address_v6`: This represents an IPv6 address
- ▶ `asio::ip::address`: This IP-protocol-version-agnostic class can represent both IPv4 and IPv6 addresses

In our sample, we use the `asio::ip::address` class, which makes the client application IP-protocol-version-agnostic. This means that it can transparently work with both IPv4 and IPv6 servers.

In step 2, we use the `asio::ip::address` class's static method, `from_string()`. This method accepts a raw IP address represented as a string, parses and validates the string, instantiates an object of the `asio::ip::address` class, and returns it to the caller. This method has four overloads. In our sample we use this one:

```
static asio::ip::address from_string(
    const std::string & str,
    boost::system::error_code & ec);
```

This method is very useful as it checks whether the string passed to it as an argument contains a valid IPv4 or IPv6 address and if it does, instantiates a corresponding object. If the address is invalid, the method will designate an error through the second argument. It means that this function can be used to validate the raw user input.

In step 3, we instantiate an object of the `boost::asio::ip::tcp::endpoint` class, passing the IP address and a protocol port number to its constructor. Now, the `ep` object can be used to designate a server application in the Boost.Asio communication related functions.

The second sample has a similar idea, although it somewhat differs from the first one. The server application is usually provided only with the protocol port number on which it should listen for incoming messages. The IP address is not provided because the server application usually wants to listen for the incoming messages on all IP addresses available on the host, not only on a specific one.

To represent the concept of *all IP addresses available on the host*, the classes `asio::ip::address_v4` and `asio::ip::address_v6` provide a static method `any()`, which instantiates a special object of corresponding class representing the concept. In step 2, we use the `any()` method of the `asio::ip::address_v6` class to instantiate such a special object.

Note that the IP-protocol-version-agnostic class `asio::ip::address` does not provide the `any()` method. The server application must explicitly specify whether it wants to receive requests either on IPv4 or on IPv6 addresses by using the object returned by the `any()` method of either the `asio::ip::address_v4` or `asio::ip::address_v6` class correspondingly. In step 2 of our second sample, we assume that our server communicates over IPv6 protocol and therefore called the `any()` method of the `asio::ip::address_v6` class.

In step 3, we create an endpoint object which represents all IP addresses available on the host and a particular protocol port number.

There's more...

In both our previous samples we used the `endpoint` class declared in the scope of the `asio::ip::tcp` class. If we look at the declaration of the `asio::ip::tcp` class, we'll see something like this:

```
class tcp
{
public:
  /// The type of a TCP endpoint.
  typedef basic_endpoint<tcp> endpoint;

  //...
}
```

It means that this `endpoint` class is a specialization of the `basic_endpoint<>` template class that is intended for use in clients and servers communicating over the TCP protocol.

However, creating endpoints that can be used in clients and servers that communicate over the UDP protocol is just as easy. To represent such an endpoint, we need to use the `endpoint` class declared in the scope of the `asio::ip::udp` class. The following code snippet demonstrates how this `endpoint` class is declared:

```
class udp
{
public:
  /// The type of a UDP endpoint.
  typedef basic_endpoint<udp> endpoint;

  //...
}
```

For example, if we want to create an endpoint in our client application to designate a server with which we want to communicate over the UDP protocol, we would only slightly change the implementation of step 3 in our sample. This is how that step would look like with changes highlighted:

```
// Step 3.
asio::ip::udp::endpoint ep(ip_address, port_num);
```

All other code would not need to be changed as it is transport protocol independent.

The same trivial change in the implementation of step 3 in our second sample is required to switch from a server communicating over TCP to one communicating over UDP.

See also

▸ The *Binding a socket to an endpoint* recipe explains how the endpoint object is used in a server application

▸ The *Connecting a socket* recipe explains how the endpoint object is used in a client application

Creating an active socket

The TCP/IP standard tells us nothing about sockets. Moreover, it tells us almost nothing about how to implement the TCP or UDP protocol software API through which this software functionality can be consumed by the application.

If we look at section 3.8, *Interface*, of the RFC document *#793* which describes the TCP protocol, we'll find out that it contains only functional requirements of a minimal set of functions that the TCP protocol software API must provide. A developer of the protocol software is given full control over all other aspects of the API, such as the structure of the API, names of the functions comprising the API, the object model, the abstractions involved, additional auxiliary functions, and so on. Every developer of the TCP protocol software is free to choose the way to implement the interface to his or her protocol implementation.

The same story applies with the UDP protocol: only a small set of functional requirements of mandatory operations are described in the RFC document *#768* devoted to it. The control of all other aspects of the UDP protocol software API is reserved for the developer of this API.

As it has already been mentioned in the introduction to this chapter, Berkeley Sockets API is the most popular TCP and UDP protocols' API. It is designed around the concept of a socket—an abstract object representing a communication session context. Before we can perform any network I/O operations, we must first allocate a socket object and then associate each I/O operation with it.

Boost.Asio borrows many concepts from Berkeley Sockets API and is so much similar to it that we can call it "an object oriented Berkeley Sockets API". The Boost.Asio library includes a class representing a socket concept, which provides interface methods similar to those found in Berkeley Sockets API.

Basically, there are two types of sockets. A socket intended to be used to send and receive data to and from a remote application or to initiate a connection establishment process with it is called an **active socket**, whereas a **passive socket** is the one used to passively wait for incoming connection requests from remote applications. Passive sockets don't take part in user data transmission. We'll talk about passive sockets later in this chapter.

This recipe explains how to create and open an active socket.

How to do it...

The following algorithm describes the steps required to perform in a client application to create and open an active socket:

1. Create an instance of the `asio::io_service` class or use the one that has been created earlier.

2. Create an object of the class that represents the transport layer protocol (TCP or UDP) and the version of the underlying IP protocol (IPv4 or IPv6) over which the socket is intended to communicate.

3. Create an object representing a socket corresponding to the required protocol type. Pass the object of `asio::io_service` class to the socket's constructor.

4. Call the socket's `open()` method, passing the object representing the protocol created in step 2 as an argument.

The following code sample demonstrates possible implementation of the algorithm. It is assumed that the socket is intended to be used to communicate over the TCP protocol and IPv4 as the underlying protocol:

```cpp
#include <boost/asio.hpp>
#include <iostream>

using namespace boost;

int main()
{
  // Step 1. An instance of 'io_service' class is required by
  // socket constructor.
  asio::io_service ios;

  // Step 2. Creating an object of 'tcp' class representing
  // a TCP protocol with IPv4 as underlying protocol.
  asio::ip::tcp protocol = asio::ip::tcp::v4();

  // Step 3. Instantiating an active TCP socket object.
  asio::ip::tcp::socket sock(ios);

  // Used to store information about error that happens
  // while opening the socket.
  boost::system::error_code ec;
```

```
    // Step 4. Opening the socket.
    sock.open(protocol, ec);

    if (ec.value() != 0) {
      // Failed to open the socket.
      std::cout
        << "Failed to open the socket! Error code = "
        << ec.value() << ". Message: " << ec.message();
        return ec.value();
    }

    return 0;
}
```

How it works...

In step 1, we instantiate an object of the `asio::io_service` class. This class is a central component in the Boost.Asio I/O infrastructure. It provides access to the network I/O services of the underlying operating system. Boost.Asio sockets get access to those services through the object of this class. Therefore, all socket class constructors require an object of `asio::io_service` as an argument. We'll consider the `asio::io_service` class in more detail in the following chapters.

In the next step, we create an instance of the `asio::ip::tcp` class. This class represents a TCP protocol. It provides no functionality, but rather acts like a data structure that contains a set of values that describe the protocol.

The `asio::ip::tcp` class doesn't have a public constructor. Instead, it provides two static methods, `asio::ip::tcp::v4()` and `asio::ip::tcp::v6()`, that return an object of the `asio::ip::tcp` class representing the TCP protocol with the underlying IPv4 or IPv6 protocol correspondingly.

Besides, the `asio::ip::tcp` class contains declarations of some basic types intended to be used with the TCP protocol. Among them are `asio::tcp::endpoint`, `asio::tcp::socket`, `asio::tcp::acceptor`, and others. Let's have a look at those declarations found in the `boost/asio/ip/tcp.hpp` file:

```
namespace boost {
namespace asio {
namespace ip {

  // ...
```

```
class tcp
{
public:
  /// The type of a TCP endpoint.
  typedef basic_endpoint<tcp> endpoint;

  // ...

  /// The TCP socket type.
  typedef basic_stream_socket<tcp> socket;

  /// The TCP acceptor type.
  typedef basic_socket_acceptor<tcp> acceptor;

  // ...
```

In step 3, we create an instance of the `asio::ip::tcp::socket` class, passing the object of the `asio::io_service` class to its constructor as an argument. Note that this constructor does not allocate the underlying operating system's socket object. The real operating system's socket is allocated in step 4 when we call the `open()` method and pass an object specifying protocol to it as an argument.

In Boost.Asio, *opening* a socket means associating it with full set of parameters describing a specific protocol over which the socket is intended to be communicating. When the Boost.Asio socket object is provided with these parameters, it has enough information to allocate a real socket object of the underlying operating system.

The `asio::ip::tcp::socket` class provides another constructor that accepts a protocol object as an argument. This constructor constructs a socket object and opens it. Note that this constructor throws an exception of the type `boost::system::system_error` if it fails. Here is a sample demonstrating how we could combine steps 3 and 4 from the previous sample:

```
try {
  // Step 3 + 4 in single call. May throw.
  asio::ip::tcp::socket sock(ios, protocol);
} catch (boost::system::system_error & e) {
  std::cout << "Error occured! Error code = " << e.code()
    << ". Message: "<< e.what();
}
```

There's more...

The previous sample demonstrates how to create an active socket intended to communicate over the TCP protocol. The process of creating a socket intended for communication over the UDP protocol is almost identical.

The following sample demonstrates how to create an active UDP socket. It is assumed that the socket is going to be used to communicate over the UDP protocol with IPv6 as the underlying protocol. No explanation is provided with the sample because it is very similar to the previous one and therefore should not be difficult to understand:

```cpp
#include <boost/asio.hpp>
#include <iostream>

using namespace boost;

int main()
{
  // Step 1. An instance of 'io_service' class is required by
  // socket constructor.
  asio::io_service ios;

  // Step 2. Creating an object of 'udp' class representing
  // a UDP protocol with IPv6 as underlying protocol.
  asio::ip::udp protocol = asio::ip::udp::v6();

  // Step 3. Instantiating an active UDP socket object.
  asio::ip::udp::socket sock(ios);

  // Used to store information about error that happens
  // while opening the socket.
  boost::system::error_code ec;

  // Step 4. Opening the socket.
  sock.open(protocol, ec);

  if (ec.value() != 0) {
    // Failed to open the socket.
    std::cout
      << "Failed to open the socket! Error code = "
      << ec.value() << ". Message: " << ec.message();
    return ec.value();
  }

  return 0;
}
```

See also

▶ The *Creating a passive socket* recipe, as its name suggests, provides discussion of passive sockets and demonstrates their use

▶ The *Connecting a socket* recipe explains one of the uses of active sockets, namely connecting to the remote application

Creating a passive socket

A passive socket or acceptor socket is a type of socket that is used to wait for connection establishment requests from remote applications that communicate over the TCP protocol. This definition has two important implications:

▶ Passive sockets are used only in server applications or hybrid applications that may play both roles of the client and server.

▶ Passive sockets are defined only for the TCP protocol. As the UDP protocol doesn't imply connection establishment, there is no need for a passive socket when communication is performed over UDP.

This recipe explains how to create and open a passive socket in Boost.Asio.

How to do it...

In Boost.Asio a passive socket is represented by the `asio::ip::tcp::acceptor` class. The name of the class suggests the key function of the objects of the class—to listen for and *accept* or handle incoming connection requests.

The following algorithm describes the steps required to perform to create an acceptor socket:

1. Create an instance of the `asio::io_service` class or use the one that has been created earlier.

2. Create an object of the `asio::ip::tcp` class that represents the TCP protocol and the required version of the underlying IP protocol (IPv4 or IPv6).

3. Create an object of the `asio::ip::tcp::acceptor` class representing an acceptor socket, passing the object of the `asio::io_service` class to its constructor.

4. Call the acceptor socket's `open()` method, passing the object representing the protocol created in step 2 as an argument.

The following code sample demonstrates the possible implementation of the algorithm. It is assumed that the acceptor socket is intended to be used over the TCP protocol and IPv6 as the underlying protocol:

```cpp
#include <boost/asio.hpp>
#include <iostream>

using namespace boost;

int main()
{
  // Step 1. An instance of 'io_service' class is required by
  // socket constructor.
  asio::io_service ios;

  // Step 2. Creating an object of 'tcp' class representing
  // a TCP protocol with IPv6 as underlying protocol.
  asio::ip::tcp protocol = asio::ip::tcp::v6();

  // Step 3. Instantiating an acceptor socket object.
  asio::ip::tcp::acceptor acceptor(ios);

  // Used to store information about error that happens
  // while opening the acceptor socket.
  boost::system::error_code ec;

  // Step 4. Opening the acceptor socket.
  acceptor.open(protocol, ec);

  if (ec.value() != 0) {
    // Failed to open the socket.
    std::cout
      << "Failed to open the acceptor socket!"
      << "Error code = "
      << ec.value() << ". Message: " << ec.message();
    return ec.value();
  }

  return 0;
}
```

How it works...

Because an acceptor socket is very similar to an active socket, the procedure of creating them is almost identical. Therefore, here we only shortly go through the sample code. For more details about each step and each object involved in the procedure, please refer to the *Creating an active socket* recipe.

In step 1, we create an instance of the `asio::io_service` class. This class is needed by all Boost.Asio components that need access to the services of the underlying operating system.

In step 2, we create an object representing a TCP protocol with IPv6 as its underlying protocol.

Then in step 3, we create an instance of the `asio::ip::tcp::acceptor` class, passing an object of the `asio::io_service` class as an argument to its constructor. Just as in the case of an active socket, this constructor instantiates an object of Boost.Asio the `asio::ip::tcp::acceptor` class, but does not allocate the actual socket object of the underlying operating system.

The operating system socket object is allocated in step 4, where we open the acceptor socket object, calling its `open()` method and passing the protocol object to it as an argument. If the call succeeds, the acceptor socket object is opened and can be used to start listening for incoming connection requests. Otherwise, the ec object of the `boost::system::error_code` class will contain error information.

See also

▸ The *Creating an active socket* recipe provides more details about the `asio::io_service` and `asio::ip::tcp` classes

Resolving a DNS name

Raw IP addresses are very inconvenient for humans to perceive and remember, especially if they are IPv6 addresses. Take a look at `192.168.10.123` (IPv4) or `8fee:9930:4545:a:105:f8ff:fe21:67cf` (IPv6). Remembering those sequences of numbers and letters could be a challenge for anyone.

To enable labeling the devices in a network with human-friendly names, the **Domain Name System** (**DNS**) was introduced. In short, DNS is a distributed naming system that allows associating human-friendly names with devices in a computer network. A **DNS name** or a **domain name** is a string that represents a name of a device in the computer network.

To be precise, a DNS name is an alias for one or more IP addresses but not the devices. It doesn't name a particular physical device but an IP address that can be assigned to a device. Thus, DNS introduces a level of indirection in addressing a particular server application in the network.

DNS acts as a distributed database storing mappings of DNS names to corresponding IP addresses and providing an interface, allowing querying the IP addresses to which a particular DNS name is mapped. The process of transforming a DNS name into corresponding IP addresses is called a **DNS name resolution**. Modern network operating systems contain functionality that can query DNS to resolve DNS names and provides the interface that can be used by applications to perform DNS name resolution.

When given a DNS name, before a client can communicate with a corresponding server application, it must first resolve the name to obtain IP addresses associated with that name.

This recipe explains how to perform a DNS name resolution with Boost.Asio.

How to do it...

The following algorithm describes steps required to perform in a client application in order to resolve a DNS name to obtain IP addresses (zero or more) of hosts (zero or more) running the server application that the client application wants to communicate with:

1. Obtain the DNS name and the protocol port number designating the server application and represent them as strings.
2. Create an instance of the `asio::io_service` class or use the one that has been created earlier.
3. Create an object of the `resolver::query` class representing a DNS name resolution query.
4. Create an instance of DNS name resolver class suitable for the necessary protocol.
5. Call the resolver's `resolve()` method, passing a query object created in step 3 to it as an argument.

The following code sample demonstrates the possible implementation of the algorithm. It is assumed that the client application is intended to communicate with the server application over the TCP protocol and IPv6 as the underlying protocol. Besides, it is assumed that the server DNS name and a port number have already been obtained and represented as strings by the client application:

```
#include <boost/asio.hpp>
#include <iostream>
```

```
using namespace boost;

int main()
{
  // Step 1. Assume that the client application has already
  // obtained the DNS name and protocol port number and
  // represented them as strings.
  std::string host = "samplehost.com";
  std::string port_num = "3333";

  // Step 2.
  asio::io_service ios;

  // Step 3. Creating a query.
  asio::ip::tcp::resolver::query resolver_query(host,
    port_num, asio::ip::tcp::resolver::query::numeric_service);

  // Step 4. Creating a resolver.
  asio::ip::tcp::resolver resolver(ios);

  // Used to store information about error that happens
  // during the resolution process.
  boost::system::error_code ec;

  // Step 5.
  asio::ip::tcp::resolver::iterator it =
    resolver.resolve(resolver_query, ec);

  // Handling errors if any.
  if (ec != 0) {
    // Failed to resolve the DNS name. Breaking execution.
    std::cout << "Failed to resolve a DNS name."
      << "Error code = " << ec.value()
      << ". Message = " << ec.message();

    return ec.value();
  }

  return 0;
}
```

How it works...

In step 1, we begin by obtaining a DNS name and a protocol port number and representing them as strings. Usually, these parameters are supplied by a user through the client application's UI or as command-line arguments. The process of obtaining and validating these parameters is behind the scope of this recipe; therefore, here we assume that they are available at the beginning of the sample.

Then, in step 2, we create an instance of the `asio::io_service` class that is used by the resolver to access underlying OS's services during a DNS name resolution process.

In step 3 we create an object of the `asio::ip::tcp::resolver::query` class. This object represents a query to the DNS. It contains a DNS name to resolve, a port number that will be used to construct an endpoint object after the DNS name resolution and a set of flags controlling some specific aspects of resolution process, represented as a bitmap. All these values are passed to the query class's constructor. Because the service is specified as a protocol port number (in our case, `3333`) and not as a service name (for example, HTTP, FTP, and so on), we passed the `asio::ip::tcp::resolver::query::numeric_service` flag to explicitly inform the query object about that, so that it properly parses the port number value.

In step 4, we create an instance of the `asio::ip::tcp::resolver` class. This class provides the DNS name resolution functionality. To perform the resolution, it requires services of the underlying operating system and it gets access to them through the object of the `asio::io_services` class being passed to its constructor as an argument.

The DNS name resolution is performed in step 5 in the resolver object's `resolve()` method. The method overload we use in our sample accepts objects of the `asio::ip::tcp::resolver::query` and `system::error_code` classes. The latter object will contain information describing the error if the method fails.

If successful, the method returns an object of the `asio::ip::tcp::resolver::iterator` class, which is an iterator pointing to the first element of a collection representing resolution results. The collection contains objects of the `asio::ip::basic_resolver_entry<tcp>` class. There are as many objects in the collection as the total number of IP addresses that resolution yielded. Each collection element contains an object of the `asio::ip::tcp::endpoint` class instantiated from one IP address resulting from the resolution process and a port number provided with the corresponding `query` object. The endpoint object can be accessed through the `asio::ip::basic_resolver_entry<tcp>::endopoint()` getter method.

The default-constructed object of the `asio::ip::tcp::resolver::iterator` class represents an end iterator. Consider the following sample demonstrating how we can iterate through the elements of the collection representing the DNS name resolution process results and how to access the resulting endpoint objects:

```
asio::ip::tcp::resolver::iterator it =
    resolver.resolve(resolver_query, ec);

asio::ip::tcp::resolver::iterator it_end;

for (; it != it_end; ++it) {
  // Here we can access the endpoint like this.
  asio::ip::tcp::endpoint ep = it->endpoint();
}
```

Usually, when a DNS name of the host running the server application is resolved to more than one IP address and correspondingly to more than one endpoint, the client application doesn't know which one of the multiple endpoints to prefer. The common approach in this case is to try to communicate with each endpoint one by one, until the desired response is received.

Note that when the DNS name is mapped to more than one IP address and some of them are IPv4 and others are IPv6 addresses, the DNS name may be resolved either to the IPv4 address or to the IPv6 address or to both. Therefore, the resulting collection may contain endpoints representing both IPv4 and IPv6 addresses.

There's more...

To resolve a DNS name and obtain a collection of endpoints that can be used in the client that is intended to communicate over the UDP protocol, the code is very similar. The sample is given here with differences highlighted and without explanation:

```
#include <boost/asio.hpp>
#include <iostream>

using namespace boost;

int main()
{
  // Step 1. Assume that the client application has already
  // obtained the DNS name and protocol port number and
  // represented them as strings.
```

```cpp
std::string host = "samplehost.book";
  std::string port_num = "3333";

  // Step 2.
  asio::io_service ios;

  // Step 3. Creating a query.
  asio::ip::udp::resolver::query resolver_query(host,
port_num, asio::ip::udp::resolver::query::numeric_service);

  // Step 4. Creating a resolver.
  asio::ip::udp::resolver resolver(ios);

  // Used to store information about error that happens
  // during the resolution process.
  boost::system::error_code ec;

  // Step 5.
  asio::ip::udp::resolver::iterator it =
    resolver.resolve(resolver_query, ec);

  // Handling errors if any.
  if (ec != 0) {
    // Failed to resolve the DNS name. Breaking execution.
    std::cout << "Failed to resolve a DNS name."
<< "Error code = " << ec.value()
<< ". Message = " << ec.message();

    return ec.value();
  }

asio::ip::udp::resolver::iterator it_end;

for (; it != it_end; ++it) {
    // Here we can access the endpoint like this.
    asio::ip::udp::endpoint ep = it->endpoint();
}

  return 0;
}
```

See also

▶ The *Creating an endpoint* recipe provides more information on endpoints

▶ For more information on DNS and domain names, refer to the specification of the system that can be found in the RFC *#1034* and RFC *#1035* documents

Binding a socket to an endpoint

Before an active socket can communicate with a remote application or a passive socket can accept incoming connection requests, they must be associated with a particular local IP address (or multiple addresses) and a protocol port number, that is, an endpoint. The process of associating a socket with a particular endpoint is called **binding**. When a socket is bound to an endpoint, all network packets coming into the host from the network with that endpoint as their target address will be redirected to that particular socket by the operating system. Likewise, all the data coming out from a socket bound to a particular endpoint will be output from the host to the network through a network interface associated with the corresponding IP address specified in that endpoint.

Some operations bind unbound sockets implicitly. For example, an operation that connects an unbound active socket to a remote application, binds it implicitly to an IP address and a protocol port number chosen by the underlying operating system. Usually, the client application doesn't need to explicitly bind an active socket to a specific endpoint just because it doesn't need that specific endpoint to communicate with the server; it only needs *any* endpoint for that purpose. Therefore, it usually delegates the right to choose the IP address and the port number to which the socket should be bound to the operating system. However, in some special cases, the client application might need to use a specific IP address and a protocol port number to communicate with the remote application and therefore will bind its socket explicitly to that specific endpoint. We wouldn't consider these cases in our book.

When socket binding is delegated to the operating system, there is no guarantee that it will be bound to the same endpoint each time. Even if there is a single network interface and a single IP address on the host, the socket may be bound to a different protocol port number every time the implicit binding is performed.

Unlike client applications that usually don't care through which IP address and protocol port number its active socket will be communicating with the remote application, the server application usually needs to bind its acceptor socket to a particular endpoint explicitly. This is explained by the fact that the server's endpoint must be known to all the clients that want to communicate with it and should stay the same after the server application is restarted.

This recipe explains how to bind a socket to particular endpoint with Boost.Asio.

How to do it...

The following algorithm describes steps required to create an acceptor socket and to bind it to an endpoint designating all IP addresses available on the host and a particular protocol port number in the IPv4 TCP server application:

1. Obtain the protocol port number on which the server should listen for incoming connection requests.

2. Create an endpoint that represents all IP addresses available on the host and the protocol port number obtained in the step 1.

3. Create and open an acceptor socket.

4. Call the acceptor socket's `bind()` method, passing the endpoint object as an argument to it.

The following code sample demonstrates possible implementation of the algorithm. It is assumed that the protocol port number has already been obtained by the application:

```cpp
#include <boost/asio.hpp>
#include <iostream>

using namespace boost;

int main()
{
  // Step 1. Here we assume that the server application has
  // already obtained the protocol port number.
  unsigned short port_num = 3333;

  // Step 2. Creating an endpoint.
  asio::ip::tcp::endpoint ep(asio::ip::address_v4::any(),
    port_num);

  // Used by 'acceptor' class constructor.
  asio::io_service ios;

  // Step 3. Creating and opening an acceptor socket.
  asio::ip::tcp::acceptor acceptor(ios, ep.protocol());

  boost::system::error_code ec;

  // Step 4. Binding the acceptor socket.
  acceptor.bind(ep, ec);
```

```
    // Handling errors if any.
    if (ec != 0) {
      // Failed to bind the acceptor socket. Breaking
      // execution.
      std::cout << "Failed to bind the acceptor socket."
        << "Error code = " << ec.value() << ". Message: "
        << ec.message();

      return ec.value();
    }

    return 0;
  }
```

How it works...

We begin by obtaining a protocol port number in step 1. The process of obtaining this parameter is beyond the scope of this recipe; therefore, here we assume that the port number has already been obtained and is available at the beginning of the sample.

In step 2 we create an endpoint representing all IP addresses available on the host and the specified port number.

In step 3 we instantiate and open the acceptor socket. The endpoint we created in step 2 contains information about the transport protocol and the version of the underlying IP protocol (IPv4). Therefore, we don't need to create another object representing the protocol to pass it to the acceptor socket's constructor. Instead, we use the endpoint's `protocol()` method, which returns an object of the `asio::ip::tcp` class representing the corresponding protocols.

The binding is performed in step 4. This is quite a simple operation. We call the acceptor socket's `bind()` method, passing an object representing an endpoint to which the acceptor socket should be bound as an argument of the method. If the call succeeds, the acceptor socket is bound to the corresponding endpoint and is ready to start listening for incoming connection requests on that endpoint.

Downloading the example code

You can download the example code files from your account at http://www.packtpub.com for all the Packt Publishing books you have purchased. If you purchased this book elsewhere, you can visit http://www.packtpub.com/support and register to have the files e-mailed directly to you.

There's more...

UDP servers don't establish connections and use active sockets to wait for incoming requests. The process of binding an active socket is very similar to binding an acceptor socket. Here, we present a sample code demonstrating how to bind a UDP active socket to an endpoint designating all IP addresses available on the host and a particular protocol port number. The code is provided without explanation:

```cpp
#include <boost/asio.hpp>
#include <iostream>

using namespace boost;

int main()
{
  // Step 1. Here we assume that the server application has
  // already obtained the protocol port number.
  unsigned short port_num = 3333;

  // Step 2. Creating an endpoint.
  asio::ip::udp::endpoint ep(asio::ip::address_v4::any(),
    port_num);

  // Used by 'socket' class constructor.
  asio::io_service ios;

  // Step 3. Creating and opening a socket.
  asio::ip::udp::socket sock(ios, ep.protocol());

  boost::system::error_code ec;

  // Step 4. Binding the socket to an endpoint.
  sock.bind(ep, ec);

  // Handling errors if any.
  if (ec != 0) {
    // Failed to bind the socket. Breaking execution.
    std::cout << "Failed to bind the socket."
      << "Error code = " << ec.value() << ". Message: "
      << ec.message();
```

```
    return ec.value();
  }

  return 0;
}
```

See also

▶ The *Creating an endpoint* recipe provides more information on endpoints

▶ The *Creating an active socket* recipe provides more details about the `asio::io_service` and `asio::ip::tcp` classes and demonstrates how to create and open an active socket

▶ The *Creating a passive socket* recipe provides information about passive sockets and demonstrates how to create and open them

Connecting a socket

Before a TCP socket can be used to communicate with a remote application, it must establish a *logical connection* with it. According to the TCP protocol, the *connection establishment process* lies in exchanging of service messages between two applications, which, if succeeds, results in two applications being *logically connected* and ready for communication with each other.

Roughly, the connection establishment process looks like this. The client application, when it wants to communicate with the server application, creates and opens an active socket and issues a `connect()` command on it, specifying a target server application with an endpoint object. This leads to a connection establishment request message being sent to the server application over the network. The server application receives the request and creates an active socket on its side, marking it as connected to a specific client and replies back to the client with the message acknowledging that connection is successfully set up on the server side. Next, the client having received the acknowledgement from the server, marks its socket as connected to the server, and sends one more message to it acknowledging that the connection is successfully set up on the client side. When the server receives the acknowledgement message from the client, the logical connection between two applications is considered established.

The point-to-point communication model is assumed between two connected sockets. This means that if socket A is connected to socket B, both can only communicate with each other and cannot communicate with any other socket C. Before socket A can communicate with socket C, it must close the connection with socket B and establish a new connection with socket C.

This recipe explains how to synchronously connect a socket to a remote application with Boost.Asio.

How to do it...

The following algorithm descries steps required to perform in the TCP client application to connect an active socket to the server application:

1. Obtain the target server application's IP address and a protocol port number.
2. Create an object of the `asio::ip::tcp::endpoint` class from the IP address and the protocol port number obtained in step 1.
3. Create and open an active socket.
4. Call the socket's `connect()` method specifying the endpoint object created in step 2 as an argument.
5. If the method succeeds, the socket is considered connected and can be used to send and receive data to and from the server.

The following code sample demonstrates a possible implementation of the algorithm:

```cpp
#include <boost/asio.hpp>
#include <iostream>

using namespace boost;

int main()
{
  // Step 1. Assume that the client application has already
  // obtained the IP address and protocol port number of the
  // target server.
  std::string raw_ip_address = "127.0.0.1";
  unsigned short port_num = 3333;

  try {
    // Step 2. Creating an endpoint designating
    // a target server application.
    asio::ip::tcp::endpoint
      ep(asio::ip::address::from_string(raw_ip_address),
      port_num);

    asio::io_service ios;

    // Step 3. Creating and opening a socket.
    asio::ip::tcp::socket sock(ios, ep.protocol());
```

```
    // Step 4. Connecting a socket.
    sock.connect(ep);

    // At this point socket 'sock' is connected to
    // the server application and can be used
    // to send data to or receive data from it.
  }
  // Overloads of asio::ip::address::from_string() and
  // asio::ip::tcp::socket::connect() used here throw
  // exceptions in case of error condition.
  catch (system::system_error &e) {
    std::cout << "Error occured! Error code = " << e.code()
      << ". Message: " << e.what();

    return e.code().value();
  }

  return 0;
}
```

How it works...

In step 1, we begin with obtaining the target server's IP address and a protocol port number. The process of obtaining these parameters is beyond the scope of this recipe; therefore, here we assume that they have already been obtained and are available at the beginning of our sample.

In step 2, we create an object of the `asio::ip::tcp::endpoint` class designating the target server application to which we are going to connect.

Then, in step 3 an active socket is instantiated and opened.

In step 4, we call the socket's `connect()` method, passing an endpoint object designating the target server to it as an argument. This function connects the socket to the server. The connection is performed synchronously, which means that the method blocks the caller thread until either the connection operation is established or an error occurs.

Note that we didn't bind the socket to any local endpoint before connecting it. This doesn't mean that the socket stays unbound. Before performing the connection establishment procedure, the socket's `connect()` method will bind the socket to the endpoint consisting of an IP address and a protocol port number chosen by the operating system.

Another thing to note in this sample is that we use an overload of the `connect()` method that throws an exception of the `boost::system::system_error` type if the operation fails, and so does overload of the `asio::ip::address::from_string()` static method we use in step 2. Therefore, both calls are enclosed in a `try` block. Both methods have overloads that don't throw exceptions and accept an object of the `boost::system::error_code` class, which is used to conduct error information to the caller in case the operation fails. However, in this case, using exceptions to handle errors makes code better structured.

There's more...

The previous code sample showed how to connect a socket to a specific server application designated by an endpoint when an IP address and a protocol port number are provided to the client application explicitly. However, sometimes the client application is provided with a DNS name that may be mapped to one or more IP addresses. In this case, we first need to resolve the DNS name using the `resolve()` method provided by the `asio::ip::tcp::resolver` class. This method resolves a DNS name, creates an object of the `asio::ip::tcp::endpoint` class from each IP address resulted from resolution, puts all endpoint objects in a collection, and returns an object of the `asio::ip::tcp::resolver::iterator` class, which is an iterator pointing to the first element in the collection.

When a DNS name resolves to multiple IP addresses, the client application—when deciding to which one to connect—usually has no reasons to prefer one IP address to any other. The common approach in this situation is to iterate through endpoints in the collection and try to connect to each of them one by one until the connection succeeds. Boost.Asio provides auxiliary functionality that implements this approach.

The free function `asio::connect()` accepts an active socket object and an object of the `asio::ip::tcp::resolver::iterator` class as input arguments, iterates over a collection of endpoints, and tries to connect the socket to each endpoint. The function stops iteration, and returns when it either successfully connects a socket to one of the endpoints or when it has tried all the endpoints and failed to connect the socket to all of them.

The following algorithm demonstrates steps required to connect a socket to a server application represented by a DNS name and a protocol port number:

1. Obtain the DNS name of a host running the server application and the server's port number and represent them as strings.

2. Resolve a DNS name using the `asio::ip::tcp::resolver` class.

3. Create an active socket without opening it.

4. Call the `asio::connect()` function passing a socket object and an iterator object obtained in step 2 to it as arguments.

The following code sample demonstrates possible implementation of the algorithm:

```cpp
#include <boost/asio.hpp>
#include <iostream>

using namespace boost;

int main()
{
  // Step1. Assume that the client application has already
  // obtained the DNS name and protocol port number and
  // represented them as strings.
  std::string host = "samplehost.book";
  std::string port_num = "3333";

  // Used by a 'resolver' and a 'socket'.
  asio::io_service ios;

  // Creating a resolver's query.
  asio::ip::tcp::resolver::query resolver_query(host, port_num,
    asio::ip::tcp::resolver::query::numeric_service);

  // Creating a resolver.
  asio::ip::tcp::resolver resolver(ios);

  try {
    // Step 2. Resolving a DNS name.
    asio::ip::tcp::resolver::iterator it =
      resolver.resolve(resolver_query);

    // Step 3. Creating a socket.
    asio::ip::tcp::socket sock(ios);

    // Step 4. asio::connect() method iterates over
    // each endpoint until successfully connects to one
    // of them. It will throw an exception if it fails
    // to connect to all the endpoints or if other
    // error occurs.
    asio::connect(sock, it);

    // At this point socket 'sock' is connected to
    // the server application and can be used
    // to send data to or receive data from it.
  }
```

```
// Overloads of asio::ip::tcp::resolver::resolve and
// asio::connect() used here throw
// exceptions in case of error condition.
catch (system::system_error &e) {
  std::cout << "Error occured! Error code = " << e.code()
    << ". Message: " << e.what();

  return e.code().value();
}

  return 0;
}
```

Note that in step 3, we don't open the socket when we create it. This is because we don't know the version of IP addresses to which the provided DNS name will resolve. The `asio::connect()` function opens the socket before connecting it to each endpoint specifying proper protocol object and closes it if the connection fails.

All other steps in the code sample should not be difficult to understand, therefore no explanation is provided.

See also

> ▸ The *Creating an endpoint* recipe provides more information on endpoints

> ▸ The *Creating an active socket* recipe explains how to create and open a socket and provides more details about the `asio::io_service` class

> ▸ The *Resolving a DNS name* recipe explains how to use a resolver class to resolve a DNS name

> ▸ The *Binding a socket* recipe provides more information about socket binding

Accepting connections

When the client application wants to communicate to the server application over a TCP protocol, it first needs to establish a logical connection with that server. In order to do that, the client allocates an active socket and issues a connect command on it (for example by calling the `connect()` method on the socket object), which leads to a connection establishment request message being sent to the server.

On the server side, some arrangements must be performed before the server application can accept and handle the connection requests arriving from the clients. Before that, all connection requests targeted at this server application are rejected by the operating system.

First, the server application creates and opens an acceptor socket and binds it to the particular endpoint. At this point, the client's connection requests arriving at the acceptor socket's endpoint are still rejected by the operating system. For the operating system to start accepting connection requests targeted at particular endpoint associated with particular acceptor socket, that acceptor socket must be switched into listening mode. After that, the operating system allocates a queue for pending connection requests associated with this acceptor socket and starts accepting connection request addressed to it.

When a new connection request arrives, it is initially received by the operating system, which puts it to the pending connection requests queue associated with an acceptor socket being the connection request's target. When in the queue, the connection request is available to the server application for processing. The server application, when ready to process the next connection request, de-queues one and processes it.

Note that the acceptor socket is only used to establish connections with client applications and is not used in the further communication process. When processing a pending connection request, the acceptor socket allocates a new active socket, binds it to an endpoint chosen by the operating system, and connects it to the corresponding client application that has issued that connection request. Then, this new active socket is ready to be used for communication with the client. The acceptor socket becomes available to process the next pending connection request.

This recipe describes how to switch an acceptor socket into listening mode and accept incoming connection requests in a TCP server application using Boost.Asio.

How to do it...

The following algorithm describes how to set up an acceptor socket so that it starts listening for incoming connections and then how to use it to synchronously process the pending connection request. The algorithm assumes that only one incoming connection will be processed in synchronous mode:

1. Obtain the port number on which the server will receive incoming connection requests.
2. Create a server endpoint.
3. Instantiate and open an acceptor socket.
4. Bind the acceptor socket to the server endpoint created in step 2.
5. Call the acceptor socket's `listen()` method to make it start listening for incoming connection requests on the endpoint.
6. Instantiate an active socket object.

7. When ready to process a connection request, call the acceptor socket's `accept()` method passing an active socket object created in step 6 as an argument.

8. If the call succeeds, the active socket is connected to the client application and is ready to be used for communication with it.

The following code sample demonstrates possible implementation of the server application that follows the algorithm. Here, we assume that the server is intended to communicate over the TCP protocol with IPv4 as the underlying protocol:

```cpp
#include <boost/asio.hpp>
#include <iostream>

using namespace boost;

int main()
{
  // The size of the queue containing the pending connection
  // requests.
  const int BACKLOG_SIZE = 30;

  // Step 1. Here we assume that the server application has
  // already obtained the protocol port number.
  unsigned short port_num = 3333;

  // Step 2. Creating a server endpoint.
  asio::ip::tcp::endpoint ep(asio::ip::address_v4::any(),
    port_num);

  asio::io_service ios;

  try {
    // Step 3. Instantiating and opening an acceptor socket.
    asio::ip::tcp::acceptor acceptor(ios, ep.protocol());

    // Step 4. Binding the acceptor socket to the
    // server endpint.
    acceptor.bind(ep);

    // Step 5. Starting to listen for incoming connection
    // requests.
    acceptor.listen(BACKLOG_SIZE);
```

```
        // Step 6. Creating an active socket.
        asio::ip::tcp::socket sock(ios);

        // Step 7. Processing the next connection request and
        // connecting the active socket to the client.
        acceptor.accept(sock);

        // At this point 'sock' socket is connected to
        //the client application and can be used to send data to
        // or receive data from it.
    }
    catch (system::system_error &e) {
        std::cout << "Error occured! Error code = " << e.code()
            << ". Message: " << e.what();

        return e.code().value();
    }

    return 0;
}
```

How it works...

In step 1, we obtain the protocol port number to which the server application binds its acceptor socket. Here, we assume that the port number has already been obtained and is available at the beginning of the sample.

In step 2, we create a server endpoint that designates all IP addresses available on the host running the server application and a specific protocol port number.

Then in step 3, we instantiate and open an acceptor socket and bind it to the server endpoint in step 4.

In step 5, we call the acceptor's `listen()` method passing the BACKLOG_SIZE constant value as an argument. This call switches the acceptor socket into the state in which it listens for incoming connection requests. Unless we call the `listen()` method on the acceptor object, all connection requests arriving at corresponding endpoint will be rejected by the operating system network software. The application must explicitly notify the operating system that it wants to start listening for incoming connection requests on specific endpoint by this call.

The argument that the `listen()` method accepts as an argument specifies the size of the queue maintained by the operating system to which it puts connection requests arriving from the clients. The requests stay in the queue and are waiting for the server application to dequeue and process them. When the queue becomes full, the new connection requests are rejected by the operating system.

In step 6, we create an active socket object without opening it. We'll need it in step 7.

In step 7, we call the acceptor socket's `accept()` method. This method accepts an active socket as an argument and performs several operations. First, it checks the queue associated with the acceptor socket containing pending connection requests. If the queue is empty, the method blocks execution until a new connection request arrives to an endpoint to which the acceptor socket is bound and the operating system puts it in the queue.

If at least one connection request is available in the queue, the one on the top of the queue is extracted from it and processed. The active socket that was passed to the `accept()` method as an argument is connected to the corresponding client application which issued the connection request.

If the connection establishment process succeeds, the `accept()` method returns and the active socket is opened and connected to the client application and can be used to send data to and receive data from it.

> Remember that the acceptor socket doesn't connect itself to the client application while processing a connection request. Instead, it opens and connects another active socket, which is then used for communication with the client application. The acceptor socket only listens for and processes (accepts) incoming connection requests.

Note that UDP servers don't use acceptor sockets because the UDP protocol doesn't imply connection establishment. Instead, an active socket is used that is bound to an endpoint and listens for incoming I/O messages, and this same active socket is used for communication.

See also

- The *Creating a passive socket* recipe provides information about passive sockets and demonstrates how to create and open them
- The *Creating an endpoint* recipe provides more information on endpoints
- The *Creating an active socket* recipe explains how to create and open a socket and provides more details about the `asio::io_service` class
- The *Binding a socket* recipe provides more information about socket binding

2

I/O Operations

In this chapter, we will cover the following recipes:

- ▶ Using fixed length I/O buffers
- ▶ Using extensible stream-oriented I/O buffers
- ▶ Writing to a TCP socket synchronously
- ▶ Reading from a TCP socket synchronously
- ▶ Writing to a TCP socket asynchronously
- ▶ Reading from a TCP socket asynchronously
- ▶ Canceling asynchronous operations
- ▶ Shutting down and closing a socket

Introduction

I/O operations are the key operations in the networking infrastructure of any distributed application. They are directly involved in the process of data exchange. Input operations are used to receive data from remote applications, whereas output operations allow sending data to them.

In this chapter, we will see several recipes that show how to perform I/O operations and other operations related to them. In addition to this, we'll see how to use some classes provided by Boost.Asio, which are used in conjunction with I/O operations.

The following is the short summary and introduction to the topics discussed in this chapter.

I/O buffers

Network programming is all about organizing inter-process communication over a computer network. **Communication** in this context implies exchanging data between two or more processes. From the perspective of a process that participates in such communication, the process performs I/O operations, sending data to and receiving it from other participating processes.

Like any other type of I/O, the network I/O involves using memory buffers, which are contiguous blocks of memory allocated in the process's address space used to store the data. When doing any sort of input operation (for example, reading some data from a file, a pipe, or a remote computer over the network), the data arrives at the process and must be stored somewhere in its address space so that it is available for further processing. That is, when the buffer comes in handy. Before performing an input operation, the buffer is allocated and then used as a data destination point during the operation. When the input operation is completed, the buffer contains input data, which can be processed by the application. Likewise, before performing the output operation, the data must be prepared and put into an output buffer, which is then used in the output operation, where it plays the role of the data source.

Apparently, the buffers are essential ingredients of any application that performs any type of I/O, including the network I/O. That's why it is critical for the developer who develops a distributed application to know how to allocate and prepare the I/O buffers to use them in the I/O operations.

Synchronous and asynchronous I/O operations

Boost.Asio supports two types of I/O operations: synchronous and asynchronous. Synchronous operations block the thread of execution invoking them and unblock only when the operation is finished. Hence, the name of this type of operation: synchronous.

The second type is an asynchronous operation. When an asynchronous operation is initiated, it is associated with a callback function or functor, which is invoked by the Boost.Asio library when the operation is finished. These types of I/O operations provide great flexibility, but may significantly complicate the code. The initiation of the operation is simple and doesn't block the thread of execution, which allows us to use the thread to run other tasks, while the asynchronous operation is being run in the background.

The Boost.Asio library is implemented as a framework, which exploits an **inversion of control** approach. After one or more asynchronous operations are initiated, the application hands over one of its threads of execution to the library, and the latter uses this thread to run the event loop and invoke the callbacks provided by the application to notify it about the completion of the previously initiated asynchronous operation. The results of asynchronous operations are passed to the callback as arguments.

Additional operations

In addition to this, we are going to consider such operations as canceling asynchronous operations, shutting down, and closing a socket.

The ability to cancel a previously initiated asynchronous operation is very important. It allows the application to state that the previously initiated operation is not relevant anymore, which may save the application's resources (both CPU and memory), that otherwise (in case, the operation would continue its execution even after it was known that nobody is interested in it anymore) would be unavoidably wasted.

Shutting down the socket is useful if there is a need for one part of the distributed application to inform the other part that the whole message has been sent, when the application layer protocol does not provide us with other means to indicate the message boundary.

As with any other operating system resource, a socket should be returned back to the operating system when it is not needed anymore by the application. A closing operation allows us to do so.

Using fixed length I/O buffers

Fixed length I/O buffers are usually used with I/O operations and play the role of either a data source or destination when the size of the message to be sent or received is known. For example, this can be a constant array of chars allocated on a stack, which contain a string that represents the request to be sent to the server. Or, this can be a writable buffer allocated in the free memory, which is used as a data destination point, when reading data from a socket.

In this recipe, we'll see how to represent fixed length buffers so that they can be used with Boost.Asio I/O operations.

How to do it...

In Boost.Asio, a fixed length buffer is represented by one of the two classes: `asio::mutable_buffer` or `asio::const_buffer`. Both these classes represent a contiguous block of memory that is specified by the address of the first byte of the block and its size in bytes. As the names of these classes suggest, `asio::mutable_buffer` represents a writable buffer, whereas `asio::const_buffer` represents a read-only one.

However, neither the `asio::mutable_buffer` nor `asio::const_buffer` classes are used in Boost.Asio I/O functions and methods directly. Instead, the `MutableBufferSequence` and `ConstBufferSequence` concepts are introduced.

The `MutableBufferSequence` concept specifies an object that represents a collection of the `asio::mutable_buffer` objects. Correspondingly, the `ConstBufferSequence` concept specifies an object that represents a collection of the `asio::const_buffer` objects. Boost.Asio functions and methods that perform I/O operations accept objects that satisfy the requirements of either the `MutableBufferSequence` or `ConstBufferSequence` concept as their arguments that represent buffers.

A complete specification of the `MutableBufferSequence` and `ConstBufferSequence` concepts are available in the Boost.Asio documentation section, which can be found at the following links:

  ▶ Refer to `http://www.boost.org/doc/libs/1_58_0/doc/html/boost_asio/reference/MutableBufferSequence.html` for `MutableBufferSequence`

  ▶ Refer to `http://www.boost.org/doc/libs/1_58_0/doc/html/boost_asio/reference/ConstBufferSequence.html` for `ConstBufferSequence`

Although in most use cases, a single buffer is involved in a single I/O operation, in some specific circumstances (for example, in a memory-constrained environment), a developer may want to use a composite buffer that comprises multiple smaller simple buffers distributed over the process's address space. Boost.Asio I/O functions and methods are designed to work with composite buffers that are represented as a collection of buffers that fulfill the requirements of either the `MutableBufferSequence` or `ConstBufferSequence` concept.

For instance, an object of the `std::vector<asio::mutable_buffer>` class satisfies the requirements of the `MutableBufferSequence` concept, and therefore, it can be used to represent a composite buffer in I/O-related functions and methods.

So, now we know that if we have a buffer that is represented as an object of the `asio::mutable_buffer` or `asio::const_buffer` class, we still can't use it with I/O-related functions or methods provided by Boost.Asio. The buffer must be represented as an object, satisfying the requirements of either the `MutableBufferSequence` or `ConstBufferSequence` concept, respectively. To do this, we for example could create a collection of buffer objects consisting of a single buffer by instantiating an object of the `std::vector<asio::mutable_buffer>` class and placing our buffer object into it. Now that the buffer is part of the collection, satisfying the `MutableBufferSequence` requirements can be used in I/O operations.

However, although this method is fine to create composite buffers consisting of two or more simple buffers, it looks overly complex when it comes to such simple tasks as representing a single simple buffer so that it can be used with Boost.Asio I/O functions or methods. Fortunately, Boost.Asio provides us with a way to simplify the usage of single buffers with I/O-related functions and methods.

The `asio::buffer()` free function has 28 overloads that accept a variety of representations of a buffer and return an object of either the `asio::mutable_buffers_1` or `asio::const_buffers_1` classes. If the buffer argument passed to the `asio::buffer()` function is a read-only type, the function returns an object of the `asio::const_buffers_1` class; otherwise, an object of the `asio::mutable_buffers_1` class is returned.

The `asio::mutable_buffers_1` and `asio::const_buffers_1` classes are *adapters* of the `asio::mutable_buffer` and `asio::const_buffer` classes, respectively. They provide an interface and behavior that satisfy the requirements of the `MutableBufferSequence` and `ConstBufferSequence` concepts, which allows us to pass these adapters as arguments to Boost.Asio I/O functions and methods.

Let's consider two algorithms and corresponding code samples that describe how to prepare a memory buffer that can be used with Boost.Asio I/O operations. The first algorithm deals with buffers intended to be used for an output operation and the second one is used for an input operation.

Preparing a buffer for an output operation

The following algorithm and corresponding code sample describes how to prepare a buffer that can be used with the Boost.Asio socket's method that performs an output operation such as `asio::ip::tcp::socket::send()` or the `asio::write()` free function:

1. Allocate a buffer. Note that this step does not involve any functionality or data types from Boost.Asio.

2. Fill the buffer with the data that is to be used as the output.

3. Represent the buffer as an object that satisfies the `ConstBufferSequence` concept's requirements.

4. The buffer is ready to be used with Boost.Asio output methods and functions.

Let's say we want to send a string `Hello` to the remote application. Before we send the data using Boost.Asio, we need to properly represent the buffer. This is how we do this in the following code:

```
#include <boost/asio.hpp>
#include <iostream>

using namespace boost;

int main()
{
  std::string buf; // 'buf' is the raw buffer.
  buf = "Hello";   // Step 1 and 2 in single line.
```

```
    // Step 3. Creating buffer representation that satisfies
    // ConstBufferSequence concept requirements.
    asio::const_buffers_1 output_buf = asio::buffer(buf);

    // Step 4. 'output_buf' is the representation of the
    // buffer 'buf' that can be used in Boost.Asio output
    // operations.

    return 0;
}
```

Preparing a buffer for an input operation

The following algorithm and corresponding code sample describes how to prepare the buffer that can be used with the Boost.Asios socket's method that performs an input operation such as `asio::ip::tcp::socket::receive()` or the `asio::read()` free function:

1. Allocate a buffer. The size of the buffer must be big enough to fit the block of data to be received. Note that this step does not involve any functionalities or data types from Boost.Asio.

2. Represent the buffer using an object that satisfies the `MutableBufferSequence` concept's requirements.

3. The buffer is ready to be used with Boost.Asio input methods and functions.

Let's say we want to receive a block of data from the server. To do this, we first need to prepare a buffer where the data will be stored. This is how we do this in the following code:

```
#include <boost/asio.hpp>
#include <iostream>
#include <memory> // For std::unique_ptr<>

using namespace boost;

int main()
{
  // We expect to receive a block of data no more than 20 bytes
  // long.
  const size_t BUF_SIZE_BYTES = 20;

  // Step 1. Allocating the buffer.
  std::unique_ptr<char[]> buf(new char[BUF_SIZE_BYTES]);
```

```
// Step 2. Creating buffer representation that satisfies
// MutableBufferSequence concept requirements.
asio::mutable_buffers_1 input_buf =
  asio::buffer(static_cast<void*>(buf.get()),
  BUF_SIZE_BYTES);

// Step 3. 'input_buf' is the representation of the buffer
// 'buf' that can be used in Boost.Asio input operations.

return 0;
}
```

How it works...

Both the samples look quite simple and straightforward; however, they contain some subtleties, which are important to understand so that we can properly use buffers with Boost.Asio. In this section, we'll see how each sample works in detail.

Preparing a buffer for an output operation

Let's consider the first code sample that demonstrates how to prepare a buffer that can be used with Boost.Asio output methods and functions. The `main()` entry point function starts with instantiating the object of the `std::string` class. Because we want to send a string of text, `std::string` is a good candidate to store this kind of data. In the next line, the string object is assigned a value of `Hello`. This is where the buffer is allocated and filled with data. This line implements steps 1 and 2 of the algorithm.

Next, before the buffer can be used with Boost.Asio I/O methods and functions, it must be properly represented. To better understand why this is needed, let's take a look at one of the Boost.Asio output functions. Here is the declaration of the `send()` method of the Boost.Asio class that represents a TCP socket:

```
template<typename ConstBufferSequence>
std::size_t send(const ConstBufferSequence & buffers);
```

As we can see, this is a template method, and it accepts an object that satisfies the requirements of the `ConstBufferSeqenece` concept as its argument that represents the buffer. A suitable object is a composite object that represents a collection of objects of the `asio::const_buffer` class and provides a typical collection interface that supports an iteration over its elements. For example, an object of the `std::vector<asio::const_buffer>` class is suitable for being used as the argument of the `send()` method, but objects of the `std::string` or `asio::const_bufer` class are not.

In order to use our `std::string` object with the `send()` method of the class that represents a TCP socket, we can do something like this:

```
asio::const_buffer asio_buf(buf.c_str(), buf.length());
std::vector<asio::const_buffer> buffers_sequence;
buffers_sequence.push_back(asio_buf);
```

The object named `buffer_sequence` in the preceding snippet satisfies the `ConstBufferSequence` concept's requirements, and therefore, it can be used as an argument for the `send()` method of the socket object. However, this approach is very complex. Instead, we use the `asio::buffer()` function provided by Boost.Asio to obtain *adaptor* objects, which we can directly use in I/O operations:

```
asio::const_buffers_1 output_buf = asio::buffer(buf);
```

After the adaptor object is instantiated, it can be used with Boost.Asio output operations to represent the output buffer.

Preparing a buffer for an input operation

The second code sample is very similar to the first one. The main difference is that the buffer is allocated but is not filled with data because its purpose is different. This time, the buffer is intended to receive the data from a remote application during the input operation.

With an output buffer, an input buffer must be properly represented so that it can be used with Boost.Asio I/O methods and functions. However, in this case, the buffer must be represented as an object that meets the requirements of the `MutableBufferSequence` concept. Contrary to `ConstBufferSequence`, this concept represents the collection of *mutable* buffers, that is, those that can be written to. Here, we use the `buffer()` function, which helps us create the required representation of the buffer. The object of the `mutable_buffers_1` adaptor class represents a single mutable buffer and meets the `MutableBufferSequence` concept's requirements.

In the first step, the buffer is allocated. In this case, the buffer is an array of chars allocated in the free memory. In the next step, the adaptor object is instantiated that can be used with both the input and output operations.

Buffer ownership

It's important to note that neither the classes that represent the buffers nor the adaptor classes provided by Boost.Asio that we've considered (namely, `asio::mutable_buffer`, `asio::const_buffer`, `asio::mutable_buffers_1`, and `asio::const_buffers_1`) take ownership of the underlying raw buffer. These classes only provide the interface to the buffer and don't control its lifetime.

See also

▶ The *Writing to a TCP socket synchronously* recipe demonstrates how to write data to the socket from a fixed-length buffer

▶ The *Reading from a TCP socket synchronously* recipe demonstrates how to read data from the socket to a fixed-length buffer

▶ The *Using composite buffers for scatter/gather operations* recipe in *Chapter 6, Other Topics*, provides more information on composite buffers and demonstrates how to use them

Using extensible stream-oriented I/O buffers

Extensible buffers are those buffers that dynamically increase their size when new data is written to them. They are usually used to read data from sockets when the size of the incoming message is unknown.

Some application layer protocols do not define the exact size of the message. Instead, the boundary of the message is represented by a specific sequence of symbols at the end of the message itself or by a transport protocol service message **end of file** (**EOF**) issued by the sender after it finishes sending the message.

For example, according to the HTTP protocol, the header section of the request and response messages don't have a fixed length and its boundary is represented by a sequence of four ASCII symbols, `<CR><LF><CR><LF>`, which is part of the message. In such cases, dynamically extensible buffers and functions that can work with them, which are provided by the Boost.Asio library, are very useful.

In this recipe, we will see how to instantiate extensible buffers and how to read and write data to and from them. To see how these buffers can be used with I/O-related methods and functions provided by Boost.Asio, refer to the corresponding recipes dedicated to I/O operations listed in the *See also* section.

How to do it...

Extensible stream-oriented buffers are represented in Boost.Asio with the `asio::streambuf` class, which is a `typedef` for `asio::basic_streambuf`:

```
typedef basic_streambuf<> streambuf;
```

The `asio::basic_streambuf<>` class is inherited from `std::streambuf`, which means that it can be used as a stream buffer for STL stream classes. In addition to this, several I/O functions provided by Boost.Asio deal with buffers that are represented as objects of this class.

We can work with an object of the `asio::streambuf` class just like we would work with any stream buffer class that is inherited from the `std::streambuf` class. For example, we can assign this object to a stream (for example, `std::istream`, `std::ostream`, or `std::iostream`, depending on our needs), and then, use stream's `operator<<()` and `operator>>()` operators to write and read data to and from the stream.

Let's consider a sample application in which an object of `asio::streambuf` is instantiated, some data is written to it, and then the data is read back from the buffer to an object of the `std::string` class:

```
#include <boost/asio.hpp>
#include <iostream>

using namespace boost;

int main()
{
  asio::streambuf buf;

  std::ostream output(&buf);

  // Writing the message to the stream-based buffer.
  output << "Message1\nMessage2";

  // Now we want to read all data from a streambuf
  // until '\n' delimiter.
  // Instantiate an input stream which uses our
  // stream buffer.
  std::istream input(&buf);

  // We'll read data into this string.
  std::string message1;

  std::getline(input, message1);

  // Now message1 string contains 'Message1'.

  return 0;
}
```

Note that this sample does not contain any network I/O operations because it focuses on the `asio::streambuf` class itself and its operations rather than on how to use this class with I/O operations.

How it works...

The `main()` application entry point function begins with instantiating an object of the `asio::streambuf` class named `buf`. Next, the output stream object of the `std::ostream` class is instantiated. The `buf` object is used as a *stream buffer* for the output stream.

In the next line, the `Message1\nMessage2` sample data string is written to the output stream object, which in turn redirects the data to the `buf` stream buffer.

Usually, in a typical client or server application, the data will be written to the `buf` stream buffer by the Boost.Asio input function such as `asio::read()`, which accepts a stream buffer object as an argument and reads data from the socket to that buffer.

Now, we want to read the data back from the stream buffer. To do this, we allocate an input stream and pass the `buf` object as a stream buffer argument to its constructor. After this, we allocate a string object named `message1`, and then, use the `std::getline` function to read part of the string currently stored in the `buf` stream buffer until the delimiter symbol, `\n`.

As a result, the `string1` object contains the `Message1` string and the `buf` stream buffer contains the rest of the initial string after the delimiter symbol, that is, `Message2`.

See also

▶ The *Reading from a TCP socket asynchronously* recipe demonstrates how to read data from the socket to an extensible stream-oriented buffer

Writing to a TCP socket synchronously

Writing to a TCP socket is an output operation that is used to send data to the remote application connected to this socket. Synchronous writing is the simplest way to send the data using a socket provided by Boost.Asio. The methods and functions that perform synchronous writing to the socket block the thread of execution and do not return until the data (at least some amount of data) is written to the socket or an error occurs.

In this recipe, we will see how to write data to a TCP socket synchronously.

How to do it...

The most basic way to write to the socket provided by the Boost.Asio library is to use the `write_some()` method of the `asio::ip::tcp::socket` class. Here is the declaration of one of the method's overloads:

```
template<
typename ConstBufferSequence>
```

```
std::size_t write_some(
const ConstBufferSequence & buffers);
```

This method accepts an object that represents a composite buffer as an argument, and as its name suggests, writes *some* amount of data from the buffer to the socket. If the method succeeds, the return value indicates the number of bytes written. The point to emphasize here is that the method may *not* send all the data provided to it through the `buffers` argument. The method only guarantees that at least one byte will be written if an error does not occur. This means that, in a general case, in order to write all the data from the buffer to the socket, we may need to call this method several times.

The following algorithm describes the steps required to synchronously write data to a TCP socket in a distributed application:

1. In a client application, allocate, open, and connect an active TCP socket. In a server application, obtain a connected active TCP socket by accepting a connection request using an acceptor socket.

2. Allocate the buffer and fill it with data that is to be written to the socket.

3. In a loop, call the socket's `write_some()` method as many times as it is needed to send all the data available in the buffer.

The following code sample demonstrates a client application, which operates according to the algorithm:

```cpp
#include <boost/asio.hpp>
#include <iostream>

using namespace boost;

void writeToSocket(asio::ip::tcp::socket& sock) {
  // Step 2. Allocating and filling the buffer.
  std::string buf = "Hello";

  std::size_t total_bytes_written = 0;

  // Step 3. Run the loop until all data is written
  // to the socket.
  while (total_bytes_written != buf.length()) {
    total_bytes_written += sock.write_some(
      asio::buffer(buf.c_str() +
      total_bytes_written,
      buf.length() - total_bytes_written));
  }
}
```

```
int main()
{
  std::string raw_ip_address = "127.0.0.1";
  unsigned short port_num = 3333;

  try {
    asio::ip::tcp::endpoint
      ep(asio::ip::address::from_string(raw_ip_address),
      port_num);

    asio::io_service ios;

// Step 1. Allocating and opening the socket.
    asio::ip::tcp::socket sock(ios, ep.protocol());

    sock.connect(ep);

    writeToSocket(sock);
  }
  catch (system::system_error &e) {
    std::cout << "Error occured! Error code = " << e.code()
      << ". Message: " << e.what();

    return e.code().value();
  }

  return 0;
}
```

Although in the presented code sample, writing to the socket is performed in the context of an application that acts as a client, the same approach can be used to write to the socket in a server application.

How it works...

The `main()` application entry point function is quite simple. It allocates a socket, opens, and synchronously connects it to a remote application. Then, the `writeToSocket()` function is called and the socket object is passed to it as an argument. In addition to this, the `main()` function contains a `try-catch` block intended to catch and handle exceptions that may be thrown by Boost.Asio methods and functions.

The interesting part in the sample is the `writeToSocket()` function that performs synchronous writing to the socket. It accepts a reference to the socket object as an argument. Its precondition is that the socket passed to it is already connected; otherwise, the function fails.

The function begins with allocating and filling the buffer. In this sample, we use an ASCII string as data that is to be written to the socket, and, therefore, we allocate an object of the `std::string` class and assign it a value of `Hello`, which we will use as a dummy message that will be written to the socket.

Then, the variable named `total_bytes_written` is defined and its value is set to `0`. This variable is used as a counter that stores the count of bytes already written to the socket.

Next, the loop is run in which the socket's `write_some()` method is called. Except for the degenerate case when the buffer is empty (that is, the `buf.length()` method returns a value of `0`), at least one iteration of the loop is executed and the `write_some()` method is called at least once. Let's take a closer look at the loop:

```
while (total_bytes_written != buf.length()) {
  total_bytes_written += sock.write_some(
    asio::buffer(buf.c_str() +
    total_bytes_written,
    buf.length() - total_bytes_written));
}
```

The termination condition evaluates to `true` when the value of the `total_bytes_written` variable is equal to the size of the buffer, that is, when all the bytes available in the buffer have been written to the socket. In each iteration of the loop, the value of the `total_bytes_written` variable is increased by the value returned by the `write_some()` method, which is equal to the number of bytes written during this method call.

Each time the `write_some()` method is called, the argument passed to it is adjusted. The start byte of the buffer is shifted by the value of `total_bytes_written` as compared to the original buffer (because the previous bytes have already been sent by preceding calls to the `write_some()` method) and the size of the buffer is decreased by the same value, correspondingly.

After the loop terminates, all the data from the buffer is written to the socket and the `writeToSocket()` function returns.

It's worth noting that the amount of bytes written to the socket during a single call to the `write_some()` method depends on several factors. In the general case, it is not known to the developer; and therefore, it should not be accounted for. A demonstrated solution is independent of this value and calls the `write_some()` method as many times as needed to write all the data available in the buffer to the socket.

Alternative – the send() method

The `asio::ip::tcp::socket` class contains another method to synchronously write data to the socket named `send()`. There are three overloads of this method. One of them is equivalent to the `write_some()` method, as described earlier. It has exactly the same signature and provides exactly the same functionality. These methods are synonyms in a sense.

The second overload accepts one additional argument as compared to the `write_some()` method. Let's take a look at it:

```
template<
typename ConstBufferSequence>
std::size_t send(
    const ConstBufferSequence & buffers,
    socket_base::message_flags flags);
```

This additional argument is named `flags`. It can be used to specify a bit mask, representing flags that control the operation. Because these flags are used quite rarely, we won't consider them in this book. Refer to the Boost.Asio documentation to find out more information on this topic.

The third overload is equivalent to the second one, but it doesn't throw exceptions in case of a failure. Instead, the error information is returned by means of an additional method's output argument of the `boost::system::error_code` type.

There's more...

Writing to a socket using the socket's `write_some()` method seems very complex for such a simple operation. Even if we want to send a small message that consists of several bytes, we must use a loop, a variable to keep track of how many bytes have already been written, and properly construct a buffer for each iteration of the loop. This approach is error-prone and makes the code more difficult to understand.

Fortunately, Boost.Asio provides a free function, which simplifies writing to a socket. This function is called `asio::write()`. Let's take a look at one of its overloads:

```
template<
    typename SyncWriteStream,
    typename ConstBufferSequence>
std::size_t write(
    SyncWriteStream & s,
    const ConstBufferSequence & buffers);
```

This function accepts two arguments. The first of them named s is a reference to an object that satisfies the requirements of the SyncWriteStream concept. For a complete list of the requirements, refer to the corresponding Boost.Asio documentation section at http://www.boost.org/doc/libs/1_58_0/doc/html/boost_asio/reference/SyncWriteStream.html. The object of the asio::ip::tcp::socket class that represents a TCP socket satisfies these requirements and, therefore, can be used as the first argument of the function. The second argument named buffers represents the buffer (simple or composite) and contains data that is to be written to the socket.

In contrast to the socket object's write_some() method, which writes *some* amount of data from the buffer to the socket, the asio::write() function writes all the data available in the buffer. This simplifies writing to the socket and makes the code shorter and cleaner.

This is how our writeToSocket() function from a previous sample would look like if we used the asio::write() function instead of the socket object's write_some() method to write data to the socket:

```
void writeToSocketEnhanced(asio::ip::tcp::socket& sock) {
  // Allocating and filling the buffer.
  std::string buf = "Hello";

  // Write whole buffer to the socket.
  asio::write(sock, asio::buffer(buf));
}
```

The asio::write() function is implemented in a similar way as the original writeToSocket() function is implemented by means of several calls to the socket object's write_some() method in a loop.

> Note that the asio::write() function has seven more overloads on the top of the one we just considered. Some of them may be very useful in specific cases. Refer to the Boost.Asio documentation to find out more about this function at http://www.boost.org/doc/libs/1_58_0/doc/html/boost_asio/reference/write.html.

See also

- The *Implementing a synchronous TCP client* recipe in *Chapter 3, Implementing Client Applications*, demonstrates how to implement a synchronous TCP client that performs synchronous writing to send request messages to the server

- The *Implementing a synchronous iterative TCP server* recipe in *Chapter 4, Implementing Server Applications*, demonstrates how to implement a synchronous TCP server that performs synchronous writing to send response messages to the client

Reading from a TCP socket synchronously

Reading from a TCP socket is an input operation that is used to receive data sent by the remote application connected to this socket. Synchronous reading is the simplest way to receive the data using a socket provided by Boost.Asio. The methods and functions that perform synchronous reading from the socket blocks the thread of execution and doesn't return until the data (at least some amount of data) is read from the socket or an error occurs.

In this recipe, we will see how to read data from a TCP socket synchronously.

How to do it...

The most basic way to read data from the socket provided by the Boost.Asio library is the `read_some()` method of the `asio::ip::tcp::socket` class. Let's take a look at one of the method's overloads:

```
template<
typename MutableBufferSequence>
std::size_t read_some(
    const MutableBufferSequence & buffers);
```

This method accepts an object that represents a writable buffer (single or composite) as an argument, and as its name suggests, reads *some* amount of data from the socket to the buffer. If the method succeeds, the return value indicates the number of bytes read. It's important to note that there is no way to control how many bytes the method will read. The method only guarantees that at least one byte will be read if an error does not occur. This means that, in a general case, in order to read a certain amount of data from the socket, we may need to call the method several times.

The following algorithm describes the steps required to synchronously read data from a TCP socket in a distributed application:

1. In a client application, allocate, open, and connect an active TCP socket. In a server application, obtain a connected active TCP socket by accepting a connection request using an acceptor socket.

2. Allocate the buffer of a sufficient size to fit in the expected message to be read.

3. In a loop, call the socket's `read_some()` method as many times as it is needed to read the message.

The following code sample demonstrates a client application, which operates according to the algorithm:

```cpp
#include <boost/asio.hpp>
#include <iostream>

using namespace boost;

std::string readFromSocket(asio::ip::tcp::socket& sock) {
  const unsigned char MESSAGE_SIZE = 7;
  char buf[MESSAGE_SIZE];
  std::size_t total_bytes_read = 0;

  while (total_bytes_read != MESSAGE_SIZE) {
    total_bytes_read += sock.read_some(
      asio::buffer(buf + total_bytes_read,
      MESSAGE_SIZE - total_bytes_read));
  }

  return std::string(buf, total_bytes_read);
}

int main()
{
  std::string raw_ip_address = "127.0.0.1";
  unsigned short port_num = 3333;

  try {
    asio::ip::tcp::endpoint
      ep(asio::ip::address::from_string(raw_ip_address),
      port_num);

    asio::io_service ios;

    asio::ip::tcp::socket sock(ios, ep.protocol());

    sock.connect(ep);

    readFromSocket(sock);
  }
  catch (system::system_error &e) {
```

```
      std::cout << "Error occured! Error code = " << e.code()
        << ". Message: " << e.what();

      return e.code().value();
   }

   return 0;
}
```

Although in the presented code sample, reading from a socket is performed in the context of an application that acts as a client, the same approach can be used to read data from the socket in a server application.

How it works...

The `main()` application entry point function is quite simple. First, it allocates a TCP socket, opens, and synchronously connects it to a remote application. Then, the `readFromSocket()` function is called and the socket object is passed to it as an argument. In addition to this, the `main()` function contains a `try-catch` block intended to catch and handle exceptions that may be thrown by Boost.Asio methods and functions.

The interesting part in the sample is the `readFromSocket()` function that performs synchronous reading from the socket. It accepts a reference to the socket object as an input argument. Its precondition is that the socket passed to it as an argument must be connected; otherwise, the function fails.

The function begins with allocating a buffer named `buf`. The size of the buffer is chosen to be 7 bytes. This is because in our sample, we expect to receive exactly a 7 bytes long message from a remote application.

Then, a variable named `total_bytes_read` is defined and its value is set to `0`. This variable is used as a counter that keeps the count of the total number of bytes read from the socket.

Next, the loop is run in which the socket's `read_some()` method is called. Let's take a closer look at the loop:

```
while (total_bytes_read != MESSAGE_SIZE) {
  total_bytes_read += sock.read_some(
    asio::buffer(buf + total_bytes_read,
    MESSAGE_SIZE - total_bytes_read));
}
```

The termination condition evaluates to `true` when the value of the `total_bytes_read` variable is equal to the size of the expected message, that is, when the whole message has been read from the socket. In each iteration of the loop, the value of the `total_bytes_read` variable is increased by the value returned by the `read_some()` method, which is equal to the number of bytes read during this method call.

Each time the `read_some()` method is called, the input buffer passed to it is adjusted. The start byte of the buffer is shifted by the value of `total_bytes_read` as compared to the original buffer (because the preceding part of the buffer has already been filled with data read from the socket during preceding calls to the `read_some()` method) and the size of the buffer is decreased by the same value, correspondingly.

After the loop terminates, all the data expected to be read from the socket is now in the buffer.

The `readFromSocket()` function ends with instantiating an object of the `std::string` class from the received buffer and returning it to the caller.

It's worth noting that the amount of bytes read from the socket during a single call to the `read_some()` method depends on several factors. In a general case, it is not known to the developer; and, therefore, it should not be accounted for. The proposed solution is independent of this value and calls the `read_some()` method as many times as needed to read all the data from the socket.

Alternative – the receive() method

The `asio::ip::tcp::socket` class contains another method to read data from the socket synchronously called `receive()`. There are three overloads of this method. One of them is equivalent to the `read_some()` method, as described earlier. It has exactly the same signature and provides exactly the same functionality. These methods are synonyms in a sense.

The second overload accepts one additional argument as compared to the `read_some()` method. Let's take a look at it:

```
template<
    typename MutableBufferSequence>
std::size_t receive(
    const MutableBufferSequence & buffers,
    socket_base::message_flags flags);
```

This additional argument is named `flags`. It can be used to specify a bit mask, representing flags that control the operation. Because these flags are rarely used, we won't consider them in this book. Refer to the Boost.Asio documentation to find out more about this topic.

The third overload is equivalent to the second one, but it doesn't throw exceptions in case of a failure. Instead, the error information is returned by means of an additional output argument of the `boost::system::error_code` type.

There's more...

Reading from a socket using the socket's `read_some()` method seems very complex for such a simple operation. This approach requires us to use a loop, a variable to keep track of how many bytes have already been read, and properly construct a buffer for each iteration of the loop. This approach is error-prone and makes the code more difficult to understand and maintain.

Fortunately, Boost.Asio provides a family of free functions that simplify synchronous reading of data from a socket in different contexts. There are three such functions, each having several overloads, that provide a rich functionality that facilitates reading data from a socket.

The asio::read() function

The `asio::read()` function is the simplest one out of the three. Let's take a look at the declaration of one of its overloads:

```
template<
    typename SyncReadStream,
    typename MutableBufferSequence>
std::size_t read(
    SyncReadStream & s,
    const MutableBufferSequence & buffers);
```

This function accepts two arguments. The first of them named s is a reference to an object that satisfies the requirements of the `SyncReadStream` concept. For a complete list of the requirements, refer to the corresponding Boost.Asio documentation section available at http://www.boost.org/doc/libs/1_58_0/doc/html/boost_asio/reference/ SyncReadStream.html. The object of the `asio::ip::tcp::socket` class that represents a TCP socket satisfies these requirements and, therefore, can be used as the first argument of the function. The second argument named `buffers` represents a buffer (simple or composite) to which the data will be read from the socket.

In contrast to the socket's `read_some()` method, which reads *some* amount of data from the socket to the buffer, the `asio::read()` function, during a single call, reads data from the socket until the buffer passed to it as an argument is filled or an error occurs. This simplifies reading from the socket and makes the code shorter and cleaner.

This is how our `readFromSocket()` function from the previous sample would look like if we used the `asio::read()` function instead of the socket object's `read_some()` method to read data from the socket:

```
std::string readFromSocketEnhanced(asio::ip::tcp::socket& sock) {
  const unsigned char MESSAGE_SIZE = 7;
  char buf[MESSAGE_SIZE];
```

```
    asio::read(sock, asio::buffer(buf, MESSAGE_SIZE));

    return std::string(buf, MESSAGE_SIZE);
}
```

In the preceding sample, a call to the `asio::read()` function will block the thread of execution until exactly 7 bytes are read or an error occurs. The benefits of this approach over the socket's `read_some()` method are obvious.

> The `asio::read()` function has several overloads, which provide flexibility in specific contexts. Refer to the corresponding section of the Boost.Asio documentation to find out more about this function at `http://www.boost.org/doc/libs/1_58_0/doc/html/boost_asio/reference/read.html`.

The asio::read_until() function

The `asio::read_until()` function provides a way to read data from a socket until a specified pattern is encountered in the data. There are eight overloads of this function. Let's consider one of them:

```
template<
    typename SyncReadStream,
    typename Allocator>
std::size_t read_until(
    SyncReadStream & s,
    boost::asio::basic_streambuf< Allocator > & b,
    char delim);
```

This function accepts three arguments. The first of them named `s` is a reference to an object that satisfies the requirements of the `SyncReadStream` concept. For a complete list of the requirements, refer to the corresponding Boost.Asio documentation section at `http://www.boost.org/doc/libs/1_58_0/doc/html/boost_asio/reference/SyncReadStream.html`. The object of the `asio::ip::tcp::socket` class that represents a TCP socket satisfies these requirements and, therefore, can be used as the first argument of the function.

The second argument named `b` represents a stream-oriented extensible buffer in which the data will be read. The last argument named `delim` specifies a delimiter character.

The `asio::read_until()` function will read data from the `s` socket to the buffer `b` until it encounters a character specified by the `delim` argument in the read portion of the data. When the specified character is encountered, the function returns.

It's important to note that the `asio::read_until()` function is implemented so that it reads the data from the socket by blocks of variable sizes (internally it uses the socket's `read_some()` method to read the data). When the function returns, the buffer b may contain some symbols after the delimiter symbol. This may happen if the remote application sends some more data after the delimiter symbol (for example, it may send two messages in a row, each having a delimiter symbol in the end). In other words, when the `asio::read_until()` function returns successfully, it is guaranteed that the buffer b contains at least one delimiter symbol but may contain more. It is the developer's responsibility to parse the data in the buffer and handle the situation when it contains data after the delimiter symbol.

This is how we will implement our `readFromSocket()` function if we want to read all the data from a socket until a specific symbol is encountered. Let's assume the message delimiter to be a new line ASCII symbol, \n:

```
std::string readFromSocketDelim(asio::ip::tcp::socket& sock) {
  asio::streambuf buf;

  // Synchronously read data from the socket until
  // '\n' symbol is encountered.
  asio::read_until(sock, buf, '\n');

  std::string message;

  // Because buffer 'buf' may contain some other data
  // after '\n' symbol, we have to parse the buffer and
  // extract only symbols before the delimiter.

  std::istream input_stream(&buf);
  std::getline(input_stream, message);
  return message;
}
```

This example is quite simple and straightforward. Because buf may contain more symbols after the delimiter symbol, we use the `std::getline()` function to extract the messages of interest before the delimiter symbol and put them into the message string object, which is then returned to the caller.

> The `read_until()` function has several overloads, which provide more sophisticated ways to specify termination conditions, such as string delimiters, regular expressions, or functors. Refer to the corresponding Boost.Asio documentation section to find out more about this topic at `http://www.boost.org/doc/libs/1_58_0/doc/html/boost_asio/reference/read_until.html`.

The asio::read_at() function

The `asio::read_at()` function provides a way to read data from a socket, starting at a particular offset. Because this function is rarely used, it is beyond the scope of this book. Refer to the corresponding Boost.Asio documentation section for more details about this function and its overloads at `http://www.boost.org/doc/libs/1_58_0/doc/html/boost_asio/reference/read_at.html`.

The `asio::read()`, `asio::read_until()`, and `asio::read_at()` functions are implemented in a similar way to how the original `readFromSocket()` function in our sample is implemented by means of several calls to the socket object's `read_some()` method in a loop until the termination condition is satisfied or an error occurs.

See also

- ▸ The *Using extensible stream-oriented I/O buffers* recipe demonstrates how to write and read data to and from the `asio::streambuf` buffer

- ▸ The *Implementing a synchronous TCP client* recipe in *Chapter 3, Implementing Client Applications*, demonstrates how to implement a synchronous TCP client that performs synchronous reading from a socket to receive response messages sent by the server

- ▸ The *Implementing a synchronous iterative TCP server* recipe in *Chapter 4, Implementing Server Applications*, demonstrates how to implement a synchronous TCP server that performs synchronous reading to receive request messages from the client

Writing to a TCP socket asynchronously

Asynchronous writing is a flexible and efficient way to send data to a remote application. In this recipe, we will see how to write data to a TCP socket asynchronously.

How to do it...

The most basic tool used to asynchronously write data to the socket provided by the Boost.Asio library is the `async_write_some()` method of the `asio::ip::tcp::socket` class. Let's take a look at one of the method's overloads:

```
template<
    typename ConstBufferSequence,
    typename WriteHandler>
void async_write_some(
    const ConstBufferSequence & buffers,
    WriteHandler handler);
```

This method initiates the write operation and returns immediately. It accepts an object that represents a buffer that contains the data to be written to the socket as its first argument. The second argument is a callback, which will be called by Boost.Asio when an initiated operation is completed. This argument can be a function pointer, functor, or any other object that satisfies the requirements of the `WriteHandler` concept. The complete list of the requirements can be found in the corresponding section of the Boost.Asio documentation at `http://www.boost.org/doc/libs/1_58_0/doc/html/boost_asio/reference/WriteHandler.html`.

The callback should have the following signature:

```
void write_handler(
    const boost::system::error_code& ec,
    std::size_t bytes_transferred);
```

Here, `ec` is an argument that indicates an error code if one occurs, and the `bytes_transferred` argument indicates how many bytes have been written to the socket during the corresponding asynchronous operation.

As the `async_write_some()` method's name suggests, it initiates an operation that is intended to write *some* amount of data from the buffer to the socket. This method guarantees that at least one byte will be written during the corresponding asynchronous operation if an error does not occur. This means that, in a general case, in order to write all the data available in the buffer to the socket, we may need to perform this asynchronous operation several times.

Now that we know how the key method works, let's see how to implement an application that performs asynchronous writing to the socket.

The following algorithm describes the steps required to perform and implement an application, which writes data to a TCP socket asynchronously. Note that this algorithm provides a *possible* way to implement such an application. Boost.Asio is quite flexible and allows us to organize and structure the application by writing data to a socket asynchronously in many different ways:

1. Define a data structure that contains a pointer to a socket object, a buffer, and a variable used as a counter of bytes written.
2. Define a callback function that will be called when the asynchronous writing operation is completed.
3. In a client application, allocate and open an active TCP socket and connect it to a remote application. In a server application, obtain a connected active TCP socket by accepting a connection request.
4. Allocate a buffer and fill it with data that is to be written to the socket.

5. Initiate an asynchronous writing operation by calling the socket's `async_write_some()` method. Specify a function defined in step 2 as a callback.

6. Call the `run()` method on an object of the `asio::io_service` class.

7. In a callback, increase the counter of bytes written. If the number of bytes written is less than the total amount of bytes to be written, initiate a new asynchronous writing operation to write the next portion of the data.

Let's implement a sample client application that performs asynchronous writing in accordance with the preceding algorithm.

We begin with adding the `include` and `using` directives:

```
#include <boost/asio.hpp>
#include <iostream>

using namespace boost;
```

Next, according to step 1 of the algorithm, we define a data structure that contains a pointer to the socket object, a buffer that contains data to be written, and a counter variable that contains the number of bytes already written:

```
// Keeps objects we need in a callback to
// identify whether all data has been written
// to the socket and to initiate next async
// writing operation if needed.
struct Session {
  std::shared_ptr<asio::ip::tcp::socket> sock;
  std::string buf;
  std::size_t total_bytes_written;
};
```

In step 2, we define a callback function, which will be called when the asynchronous operation is completed:

```
// Function used as a callback for
// asynchronous writing operation.
// Checks if all data from the buffer has
// been written to the socket and initiates
// new asynchronous writing operation if needed.
void callback(const boost::system::error_code& ec,
        std::size_t bytes_transferred,
        std::shared_ptr<Session> s)
{
```

```
    if (ec != 0) {
      std::cout << "Error occured! Error code = "
      << ec.value()
      << ". Message: " << ec.message();

      return;
    }

    s->total_bytes_written += bytes_transferred;

    if (s->total_bytes_written == s->buf.length()) {
      return;
    }

    s->sock->async_write_some(
    asio::buffer(
    s->buf.c_str() +
    s->total_bytes_written,
    s->buf.length() -
    s->total_bytes_written),
    std::bind(callback, std::placeholders::_1,
    std::placeholders::_2, s));
  }
```

Let's skip step 3 for now and implement steps 4 and 5 in a separate function. Let's call this function writeToSocket():

```
  void writeToSocket(std::shared_ptr<asio::ip::tcp::socket> sock) {

    std::shared_ptr<Session> s(new Session);

    // Step 4. Allocating and filling the buffer.
    s->buf = std::string("Hello");
    s->total_bytes_written = 0;
    s->sock = sock;

    // Step 5. Initiating asynchronous write operation.
    s->sock->async_write_some(
    asio::buffer(s->buf),
    std::bind(callback,
    std::placeholders::_1,
    std::placeholders::_2,
    s));
  }
```

Now, we come back to step 3 and implement it in the `main()` application entry point function:

```cpp
int main()
{
  std::string raw_ip_address = "127.0.0.1";
  unsigned short port_num = 3333;

  try {
    asio::ip::tcp::endpoint
      ep(asio::ip::address::from_string(raw_ip_address),
      port_num);

    asio::io_service ios;

    // Step 3. Allocating, opening and connecting a socket.
    std::shared_ptr<asio::ip::tcp::socket> sock(
    new asio::ip::tcp::socket(ios, ep.protocol()));

    sock->connect(ep);

    writeToSocket(sock);

    // Step 6.
    ios.run();
  }
  catch (system::system_error &e) {
    std::cout << "Error occured! Error code = " << e.code()
      << ". Message: " << e.what();

    return e.code().value();
  }

  return 0;
}
```

How it works...

Now, let's track the application's execution path to better understand how it works.

The application is run by a single thread, in the context of which the application's `main()` entry point function is called. Note that Boost.Asio may create additional threads for some internal operations, but it guarantees that no application code is executed in the context of those threads.

The `main()` function allocates, opens, and synchronously connects a socket to a remote application and then calls the `writeToSocket()` function by passing a pointer to the socket object. This function initiates an asynchronous write operation and returns. We'll consider this function in a moment. The `main()` function continues with calling the `run()` method on the object of the `asio::io_service` class, where Boost.Asio *captures* the thread of execution and uses it to call the callback functions associated with asynchronous operations when they get completed.

The `asio::os_service::run()` method blocks, as long as, at least one pending asynchronous operation. When the last callback of the last pending asynchronous operation is completed, this method returns.

Now, let's come back to the `writeToSocket()` function and analyze its behavior. It begins with allocating an instance of the `Session` data structure in the free memory. Then, it allocates and fills the buffer with the data to be written to the socket. After this, a pointer to the socket object and the buffer are stored in the `Session` object. Because the socket's `async_write_some()` method may not write all the data to the socket in one go, we may need to initiate another asynchronous write operation in a callback function. That's why we need the `Session` object and we allocate it in the free memory and not on the stack; it must *live* until the callback function is called.

Finally, we initiate the asynchronous operation, calling the socket object's `async_write_some()` method. The invocation of this method is somewhat complex, and, therefore, let's consider this in more detail:

```
s->sock->async_write_some(
   asio::buffer(s->buf),
   std::bind(callback,
       std::placeholders::_1,
 std::placeholders::_2,
   s));
```

The first argument is a buffer that contains data to be written to the socket. Because the operation is asynchronous, this buffer may be accessed by Boost.Asio at any moment between operation initiation and when the callback is called. This means that the buffer must stay intact and must be available until the callback is called. We guarantee this by storing the buffer in a `Session` object, which in turn is stored in the free memory.

The second argument is a callback that is to be invoked when the asynchronous operation is completed. Boost.Asio defines a callback as a *concept*, which can be a function or a functor, that accepts two arguments. The first argument of the callback specifies an error that occurs while the operation is being executed, if any. The second argument specifies the number of bytes written by the operation.

Because we want to pass an additional argument to our callback function, a pointer to the corresponding `Session` object, which acts as a context for the operation, we use the `std::bind()` function to construct a function object to which we attach a pointer to the `Session` object as the third argument. The function object is then passed as a callback argument to the socket object's `async_write_some()` method.

Because it is asynchronous, the `async_write_some()` method doesn't block the thread of execution. It initiates the writing operation and returns.

The actual writing operation is executed behind the scenes by the Boost.Asio library and underlying operating system, and when the operation is complete or an error occurs, the callback is invoked.

When invoked, the callback function named, literally, `callback` in our sample application begins with checking whether the operation succeeded or an error occurred. In the latter case, the error information is output to the standard output stream and the function returns. Otherwise, the counter of the total written bytes is increased by the number of bytes written as a result of an operation. Then, we check whether the total number of bytes written to the socket is equal to the size of the buffer. If these values are equal, this means that all the data has been written to the socket and there is no more work to do. The callback function returns. However, if there is still data in the buffer that is to be written, a new asynchronous write operation is initiated:

```
s->sock->async_write_some(
asio::buffer(
s->buf.c_str() +
s->total_bytes_written,
s->buf.length() -
s->total_bytes_written),
std::bind(callback, std::placeholders::_1,
std::placeholders::_2, s));
```

Note how the beginning of the buffer is shifted by the number of bytes already written, and how the size of the buffer is decreased by the same value, correspondingly.

As a callback, we specify the same `callback()` function using the `std::bind()` function to attach an additional argument—the `Session` object, just like we did when we initiated the first asynchronous operation.

The cycles of initiation of an asynchronous writing operation and consequent callback invocation repeat until all the data from the buffer is written to the socket or an error occurs.

When the `callback` function returns without initiating a new asynchronous operation, the `asio::io_service::run()` method, called in the `main()` function, unblocks the thread of execution and returns. The `main()` function returns as well. This is when the application exits.

There's more...

Although the `async_write_some()` method described in the previous sample allows asynchronously writing data to the socket, the solution based on it is somewhat complex and error-prone. Fortunately, Boost.Asio provides a more convenient way to asynchronously write data to a socket using the free function `asio::async_write()`. Let's consider one of its overloads:

```
template<
    typename AsyncWriteStream,
    typename ConstBufferSequence,
    typename WriteHandler>
void async_write(
    AsyncWriteStream & s,
    const ConstBufferSequence & buffers,
    WriteHandler handler);
```

This function is very similar to the socket's `async_write_some()` method. Its first argument is an object that satisfies the requirements of the `AsyncWriteStream` concept. For the complete list of the requirements, refer to the corresponding Boost.Asio documentation section at `http://www.boost.org/doc/libs/1_58_0/doc/html/boost_asio/reference/AsyncWriteStream.html`. The object of the `asio::ip::tcp::socket` class satisfies these requirements and, therefore, can be used with this function.

The second and the third arguments of the `asio::async_write()` function are similar to the first and second arguments of the `async_write_some()` method of a TCP socket object described in the previous sample. These arguments are buffers that contain data that is to be written and functions or objects that represent a callback, which will be called when the operation is completed.

In contrast to the socket's `async_write_some()` method, which initiates the operation that writes *some* amount of data from the buffer to the socket, the `asio::async_write()` function initiates the operation, which writes all the data available in the buffer. In this case, the callback is called only when all the data available in the buffer is written to the socket or when an error occurs. This simplifies writing to the socket and makes the code shorter and cleaner.

If we change our previous sample so that it uses the `asio::async_write()` function instead of the socket object's `async_write_some()` method to write data to the socket asynchronously, our application becomes significantly simpler.

Firstly, we don't need to keep track of the number of bytes written to the socket, so therefore, the `Session` structure becomes smaller:

```
struct Session {
  std::shared_ptr<asio::ip::tcp::socket> sock;
  std::string buf;
};
```

Secondly, we know that when the callback function is invoked, it means that either all the data from the buffer has been written to the socket or an error has occurred. This makes the callback function much simpler:

```
void callback(const boost::system::error_code& ec,
  std::size_t bytes_transferred,
  std::shared_ptr<Session> s)
{
  if (ec != 0) {
    std::cout << "Error occured! Error code = "
      << ec.value()
      << ". Message: " << ec.message();

    return;
  }

  // Here we know that all the data has
  // been written to the socket.
}
```

The `asio::async_write()` function is implemented by means of zero or more calls to the socket object's `async_write_some()` method. This is similar to how the `writeToSocket()` function in our initial sample is implemented.

> Note that the `asio::async_write()` function has three more overloads, providing additional functionalities. Some of them may be very useful in specific circumstances. Refer to the Boost.Asio documentation to find out more about this function at `http://www.boost.org/doc/libs/1_58_0/doc/html/boost_asio/reference/async_write.html`.

See also

▶ The *Writing to a TCP socket synchronously* recipe describes how to write data to a TCP socket synchronously

▶ The *Implementing an asynchronous TCP client* recipe in *Chapter 3, Implementing Client Applications*, demonstrates how to implement an asynchronous TCP client that performs asynchronous writing to a TCP socket to send request messages to the server

▶ The *Implementing an asynchronous TCP server* recipe in *Chapter 4, Implementing Server Applications*, demonstrates how to implement an asynchronous TCP server that performs asynchronous writing to a TCP socket to send response messages to the client

Reading from a TCP socket asynchronously

Asynchronous reading is a flexible and efficient way to receive data from a remote application. In this recipe, we will see how to read data from a TCP socket asynchronously.

How to do it...

The most basic tool used to asynchronously read data from a TCP socket provided by the Boost.Asio library is the `async_read_some()` method of the `asio::ip::tcp::socket` class. Here is one of the method's overloads:

```
template<
    typename MutableBufferSequence,
    typename ReadHandler>
void async_read_some(
    const MutableBufferSequence & buffers,
    ReadHandler handler);
```

This method initiates an asynchronous read operation and returns immediately. It accepts an object that represents a mutable buffer as its first argument to which the data will be read from the socket. The second argument is a callback that is called by Boost.Asio when the operation is completed. This argument can be a function pointer, a functor, or any other object that satisfies the requirements of the `ReadHandler` concept. The complete list of the requirements can be found in the corresponding section of the Boost.Asio documentation at http://www.boost.org/doc/libs/1_58_0/doc/html/boost_asio/reference/ ReadHandler.html.

The callback should have the following signature:

```
void read_handler(
    const boost::system::error_code& ec,
    std::size_t bytes_transferred);
```

Here, `ec` is an argument that notifies an error code if one occurs, and the `bytes_transferred` argument indicates how many bytes have been read from the socket during the corresponding asynchronous operation.

As the `async_read_some()` method's name suggests, it initiates an operation that is intended to read *some* amount of data from the socket to the buffer. This method guarantees that at least one byte will be read during the corresponding asynchronous operation if an error does not occur. This means that, in a general case, in order to read all the data from the socket, we may need to perform this asynchronous operation several times.

Now that we know how the key method works, let's see how to implement an application that performs asynchronous reading from the socket.

The following algorithm describes the steps required to implement an application, which reads data from a socket asynchronously. Note that this algorithm provides a *possible* way to implement such an application. Boost.Asio is quite flexible and allows us to organize and structure the application by reading data from a socket asynchronously in different ways:

1. Define a data structure that contains a pointer to a socket object, a buffer, a variable that defines the size of the buffer, and a variable used as a counter of bytes read.

2. Define a callback function that will be called when an asynchronous reading operation is completed.

3. In a client application, allocate and open an active TCP socket, and then, connect it to a remote application. In a server application, obtain a connected active TCP socket by accepting a connection request.

4. Allocate a buffer big enough for the expected message to fit in.

5. Initiate an asynchronous reading operation by calling the socket's `async_read_some()` method, specifying a function defined in step 2 as a callback.

6. Call the `run()` method on an object of the `asio::io_service` class.

7. In a callback, increase the counter of bytes read. If the number of bytes read is less than the total amount of bytes to be read (that is, the size of an expected message), initiate a new asynchronous reading operation to read the next portion of data.

Let's implement a sample client application which will perform asynchronous reading in accordance with the preceding algorithm.

We begin with adding the `include` and `using` directives:

```
#include <boost/asio.hpp>
#include <iostream>

using namespace boost;
```

Next, according to step 1, we define a data structure that contains a pointer to the socket object named `sock`, a pointer to the buffer named `buf`, a variable named `buf_size` that contains the size of the buffer, and a `total_bytes_read` variable that contains the number of bytes already read:

```
// Keeps objects we need in a callback to
// identify whether all data has been read
// from the socket and to initiate next async
// reading operation if needed.
struct Session {
  std::shared_ptr<asio::ip::tcp::socket> sock;
  std::unique_ptr<char[]> buf;
  std::size_t total_bytes_read;
  unsigned int buf_size;
};
```

In step 2, we define a callback function, which will be called when asynchronous operation is completed:

```
// Function used as a callback for
// asynchronous reading operation.
// Checks if all data has been read
// from the socket and initiates
// new reading operation if needed.
void callback(const boost::system::error_code& ec,
  std::size_t bytes_transferred,
  std::shared_ptr<Session> s)
{
  if (ec != 0) {
    std::cout << "Error occured! Error code = "
      << ec.value()
      << ". Message: " << ec.message();

    return;
  }
```

```
    s->total_bytes_read += bytes_transferred;

    if (s->total_bytes_read == s->buf_size) {
      return;
    }

    s->sock->async_read_some(
      asio::buffer(
      s->buf.get() +
        s->total_bytes_read,
      s->buf_size -
        s->total_bytes_read),
      std::bind(callback, std::placeholders::_1,
      std::placeholders::_2, s));
  }
```

Let's skip step 3 for now and implement steps 4 and 5 in a separate function. Let's name this function readFromSocket():

```
  void readFromSocket(std::shared_ptr<asio::ip::tcp::socket> sock) {
    std::shared_ptr<Session> s(new Session);

    // Step 4. Allocating the buffer.
    const unsigned int MESSAGE_SIZE = 7;

    s->buf.reset(new char[MESSAGE_SIZE]);
    s->total_bytes_read = 0;
    s->sock = sock;
    s->buf_size = MESSAGE_SIZE;

    // Step 5. Initiating asynchronous reading operation.
    s->sock->async_read_some(
      asio::buffer(s->buf.get(), s->buf_size),
      std::bind(callback,
        std::placeholders::_1,
        std::placeholders::_2,
        s));
  }
```

Now, we come back to step 3 and implement it in the application's main() entry point function:

```
  int main()
  {
    std::string raw_ip_address = "127.0.0.1";
```

```
    unsigned short port_num = 3333;

    try {
      asio::ip::tcp::endpoint
        ep(asio::ip::address::from_string(raw_ip_address),
        port_num);

      asio::io_service ios;

      // Step 3. Allocating, opening and connecting a socket.
      std::shared_ptr<asio::ip::tcp::socket> sock(
        new asio::ip::tcp::socket(ios, ep.protocol()));

      sock->connect(ep);

      readFromSocket(sock);

      // Step 6.
      ios.run();
    }
    catch (system::system_error &e) {
      std::cout << "Error occured! Error code = " << e.code()
        << ". Message: " << e.what();

      return e.code().value();
    }

    return 0;
}
```

How it works...

Now, let's track the application's execution path to better understand how it works.

The application is run by a single thread; in the context of which the application's main() entry point function is called. Note that Boost.Asio may create additional threads for some internal operations, but it guarantees that no application code is called in the context of those threads.

The `main()` function begins with allocating, opening, and connecting a socket to a remote application. Then, it calls the `readFromSocket()` function and passes a pointer to the socket object as an argument. The `readFromSocket()` function initiates an asynchronous reading operation and returns. We'll consider this function in a moment. The `main()` function continues with calling the `run()` method on the object of the `asio::io_service` class, where Boost.Asio *captures* the thread of execution and uses it to call the callback functions associated with asynchronous operations when they get completed.

The `asio::io_service::run()` method blocks as long as there is at least one pending asynchronous operation. When the last callback of the last pending operation is completed, this method returns.

Now, let's come back to the `readFromSocket()` function and analyze its behavior. It begins with allocating an instance of the `Session` data structure in the free memory. Then, it allocates a buffer and stores a pointer to it in a previously allocated instance of the `Session` data structure. A pointer to the socket object and the size of the buffer are stored in the `Session` data structure as well. Because the socket's `async_read_some()` method may not read all the data in one go, we may need to initiate another asynchronous reading operation in the callback function. This is why we need the `Session` data structure and why we allocate it in the free memory and not on a stack. This structure and all the objects that reside in it must *live* at least until the callback is invoked.

Finally, we initiate the asynchronous operation, calling the socket object's `async_read_some()` method. The invocation of this method is somewhat complex; therefore, let's take a look at it in more detail:

```
s->sock->async_read_some(
    asio::buffer(s->buf.get(), s->buf_size),
    std::bind(callback,
        std::placeholders::_1,
        std::placeholders::_2,
        s));
```

The first argument is the buffer to which the data will be read. Because the operation is asynchronous, this buffer may be accessed by Boost.Asio at any moment between the operation initiation and when the callback is invoked. This means that the buffer must stay intact and be available until the callback is invoked. We guarantee this by allocating the buffer in the free memory and storing it in the `Session` data structure, which in turn is allocated in the free memory as well.

The second argument is a callback that is to be invoked when the asynchronous operation is completed. Boost.Asio defines a callback as a concept, which can be a function or a functor, that accepts two arguments. The first argument of the callback specifies an error that occurs while the operation is being executed, if any. The second argument specifies the number of bytes read by the operation.

Because we want to pass an additional argument to our callback function, a pointer to the corresponding `Session` object, which serves as a context for the operation—we use the `std::bind()` function to construct a function object to which we attach a pointer to the `Session` object as the third argument. The function object is then passed as a callback argument to the socket object's `async_write_some()` method.

Because it is asynchronous, the `async_write_some()` method doesn't block the thread of execution. It initiates the reading operation and returns.

The actual reading operation is executed behind the scenes by the Boost.Asio library and underlying operating system, and when the operation is completed or an error occurs, the callback is invoked.

When invoked, the callback function named, literally, `callback` in our sample application begins with checking whether the operation succeeded or an error occurred. In the latter case, the error information is output to the standard output stream and the function returns. Otherwise, the counter of the total read bytes is increased by the number of bytes read as a result of the operation. Then, we check whether the total number of bytes read from the socket is equal to the size of the buffer. If these values are equal, it means that the buffer is full and there is no more work to do. The callback function returns. However, if there is still some space in the buffer, we need to continue with reading; therefore, we initiate a new asynchronous reading operation:

```
s->sock->async_read_some(
    asio::buffer(s->buf.get(), s->buf_size),
    std::bind(callback,
        std::placeholders::_1,
        std::placeholders::_2,
        s));
```

Note that the beginning of the buffer is shifted by the number of bytes already read and the size of the buffer is decreased by the same value, respectively.

As a callback, we specify the same `callback` function using the `std::bind()` function to attach an additional argument—the `Session` object.

The cycles of initiation of an asynchronous reading operation and consequent callback invocation repeat until the buffer is full or an error occurs.

When the `callback` function returns without initiating a new asynchronous operation, the `asio::io_service::run()` method, called in the `main()` function, unblocks the thread of execution and returns. The `main()` function returns as well. This is when the application exits.

There's more...

Although the `async_read_some()` method, as described in the previous sample, allows asynchronously reading data from the socket, the solution based on it is somewhat complex and error-prone. Fortunately, Boost.Asio provides a more convenient way to asynchronously read data from a socket: the free function `asio::async_read()`. Let's consider one of its overloads:

```
template<
    typename AsyncReadStream,
    typename MutableBufferSequence,
    typename ReadHandler>
void async_read(
    AsyncReadStream & s,
    const MutableBufferSequence & buffers,
    ReadHandler handler);
```

This function is very similar to the socket's `async_read_some()` method. Its first argument is an object that satisfies the requirements of the `AsyncReadStream` concept. For the complete list of the requirements, refer to the corresponding Boost.Asio documentation section at `http://www.boost.org/doc/libs/1_58_0/doc/html/boost_asio/reference/AsyncReadStream.html`. The object of the `asio::ip::tcp::socket` class satisfies these requirements and, therefore, can be used with this function.

The second and third arguments of the `asio::async_read()` function are similar to the first and second arguments of the `async_read_some()` method of a TCP socket object described in the previous sample. These arguments are buffers used as data destination points and functions or objects that represent a callback, which will be called when the operation is completed.

In contrast to the socket's `async_read_some()` method, which initiates the operation, that reads *some* amount of data from the socket to the buffer, the `asio::async_read()` function initiates the operation that reads the data from the socket until the buffer passed to it as an argument is full. In this case, the callback is called when the amount of data read is equal to the size of the provided buffer or when an error occurs. This simplifies reading from the socket and makes the code shorter and cleaner.

If we change our previous sample so that it uses the `asio::async_read()` function instead of the socket object's `async_read_some()` method to read data from the socket asynchronously, our application becomes significantly simpler.

Firstly, we don't need to keep track of the number of bytes read from the socket; therefore, the `Session` structure becomes smaller:

```
struct Session {
  std::shared_ptr<asio::ip::tcp::socket> sock;
  std::unique_ptr<char[]> buf;
  unsigned int buf_size;
};
```

Secondly, we know that when the callback function is invoked, it means that either an expected amount of data has been read from the socket or an error has occurred. This makes the callback function much simpler:

```
void callback(const boost::system::error_code& ec,
  std::size_t bytes_transferred,
  std::shared_ptr<Session> s)
{
  if (ec != 0) {
    std::cout << "Error occured! Error code = "
      << ec.value()
      << ". Message: " << ec.message();

    return;
  }

  // Here we know that the reading has completed
  // successfully and the buffer is full with
  // data read from the socket.
}
```

The `asio::async_read()` function is implemented by means of zero or more calls to the socket object's `async_read_some()` method. This is similar to how the `readFromSocket()` function in our initial sample is implemented.

 Note that the `asio::async_read()` function has three more overloads, providing additional functionalities. Some of them may be very useful in specific circumstances. Refer to the Boost.Asio documentation to find out about this at `http://www.boost.org/doc/libs/1_58_0/doc/html/boost_asio/reference/async_read.html`.

See also

- ▶ The *Reading from a TCP socket synchronously* recipe describes how to read data from a TCP socket synchronously

- ▶ The *Implementing an asynchronous TCP client* recipe in *Chapter 3, Implementing Client Applications*, demonstrates how to implement an asynchronous TCP client that performs asynchronous reading from a TCP socket to receive response messages sent by the server

- ▶ The *Implementing an asynchronous TCP server* recipe in *Chapter 4, Implementing Server Applications*, demonstrates how to implement an asynchronous TCP server that performs asynchronous reading from a TCP socket to receive request messages from the client

Canceling asynchronous operations

Sometimes, after an asynchronous operation has been initiated and has not yet completed, the conditions in the application may change so that the initiated operation becomes irrelevant or outdated and nobody is interested in the completion of the operation.

In addition to this, if an initiated asynchronous operation is a reaction to a user command, the user may change their mind while the operation is being executed. The user may want to discard the previous issued command and may want to issue a different one or decide to exit from the application.

Consider a situation where a user types a website address in a typical web browser's address bar and hits the *Enter* key. The browser immediately initiates a DNS name resolution operation. When the DNS name is resolved and the corresponding IP address is obtained, it initiates the connection operation to connect to the corresponding web server. When a connection is established, the browser initiates an asynchronous write operation to send a request to the server. Finally, when the request is sent, the browser starts waiting for the response message. Depending on the responsiveness of the server application, the volume of the data transmitted over the network, the state of the network, and other factors, all these operations may take a substantial amount of time. And the user while waiting for the requested web page to be loaded, may change their mind, and before the page gets loaded, the user may type another website address in the address bar and hit *Enter*.

Another (extreme) situation is where a client application sends a request to the server application and starts waiting for the response message, but the server application while processing the client's request, gets into a deadlock due to bugs in it. In this case, the user would have to wait forever for the response message and would never get it.

In both the cases, the user of the client application would benefit from having the ability to cancel the operation they initiated before it completes. In general, it is a good practice to provide the user with the ability to cancel an operation that may take a noticeable amount of time. Because the network communication operations fall into a class of operations that may last for unpredictably long periods of time, it is important to support the cancelation of operations in distributed applications that communicate over the network.

One of the benefits of asynchronous operations provided by the Boost.Asio library is that they can be canceled at any moment after the initiation. In this recipe, we'll see how to cancel asynchronous operations.

How to do it...

The following algorithm provides the steps required to initiate and cancel asynchronous operations with Boost.Asio:

1. If the application is intended to run on Windows XP or Windows Server 2003, define flags that enable asynchronous operation canceling on these versions of Windows.

2. Allocate and open a TCP or UDP socket. It may be an active or passive (acceptor) socket in the client or server application.

3. Define a callback function or functor for an asynchronous operation. If needed, in this callback, implement a branch of code that handles the situation when the operation has been canceled.

4. Initiate one or more asynchronous operations and specify a function or an object defined in step 4 as a callback.

5. Spawn an additional thread and use it to run the Boost.Asio event loop.

6. Call the `cancel()` method on the socket object to cancel all the outstanding asynchronous operations associated with this socket.

Let's consider the implementation of the client application designed in accordance with the presented algorithm in which an asynchronous *connection* operation is first initiated and then canceled.

According to step 1, to compile and run our code on Windows XP or Windows Server 2003, we need to define some flags that control the behavior of the Boost.Asio library with regard to which mechanisms of the underlying OS to exploit.

By default, when it is compiled for Windows, Boost.Asio uses the I/O completion port framework to run operations asynchronously. On Windows XP and Windows Server 2003, this framework has some issues and limitations with regard to the cancelation of an operation. Therefore, Boost.Asio requires developers to explicitly notify that they want to enable the asynchronous operation canceling functionality despite of the known issues, when targeting the application in versions of Windows in question. To do this, the `BOOST_ASIO_ENABLE_CANCELIO` macro must be defined before Boost.Asio headers are included. Otherwise, if this macro is not defined, while the source code of the application contains calls to asynchronous operations, cancelation methods and functions, the compilation will always fail.

In other words, it is mandatory to define the `BOOST_ASIO_ENABLE_CANCELIO` macro, when targeting Windows XP or Windows Server 2003, and the application needs to cancel asynchronous operations.

To get rid of issues and limitations imposed by the usage of the I/O completion port framework on Windows XP and Windows Server 2003, we can prevent Boost.Asio from using this framework by defining another macro named `BOOST_ASIO_DISABLE_IOCP` before including Boost.Asio headers. With this macro defined, Boost.Asio doesn't use the I/O completion port framework on Windows; and therefore, problems related to asynchronous operations canceling disappear. However, the benefits of scalability and efficiency of the I/O completion ports framework disappear too.

Note that the mentioned issues and limitations related to asynchronous operation canceling do not exist on Windows Vista and Windows Server 2008 and later. Therefore, when targeting these versions of Windows, canceling works fine, and there is no need to disable the I/O completion port framework usage unless there is another reason to do so. Refer to the `asio::ip::tcp::cancel()` method's documentation section for more details on this issue at `http://www.boost.org/doc/libs/1_58_0/doc/html/boost_asio/reference/basic_stream_socket/cancel/overload1.html`.

In our sample, we will consider how to construct a cross-platform application that, when targeted at Windows during compilation, can be run on any Windows version, starting from Windows XP or Windows Server 2003. Therefore, we define both the `BOOST_ASIO_DISABLE_IOCP` and `BOOST_ASIO_ENABLE_CANCELIO` macros.

To determine the target operating system at compile time, we use the `Boost.Predef` library. This library provides us with macro definitions that allow us to identify parameters of the environment in which the code is compiled as the target operating system family and its version, processor architecture, compiler, and many others. Refer to the Boost.Asio documentation section for more details on this library at `http://www.boost.org/doc/libs/1_58_0/libs/predef/doc/html/index.html`.

To use the `Boost.Predef` library, we include the following header file:

```
#include <boost/predef.h> // Tools to identify the OS.
```

Then, we check whether the code is being compiled for Windows XP or Windows Server 2003, and if it is, we define the BOOST_ASIO_DISABLE_IOCP and BOOST_ASIO_ENABLE_ CANCELIO macros:

```
#ifdef BOOST_OS_WINDOWS
#define _WIN32_WINNT 0x0501

#if _WIN32_WINNT <= 0x0502 // Windows Server 2003 or earlier.
#define BOOST_ASIO_DISABLE_IOCP
#define BOOST_ASIO_ENABLE_CANCELIO
#endif
#endif
```

Next, we include the common Boost.Asio header and standard library <thread> header. We will need the latter because we'll spawn additional threads in our application. In addition to this, we specify a using directive to make the names of Boost.Asio classes and functions shorter and more convenient to use:

```
#include <boost/asio.hpp>
#include <iostream>
#include <thread>

using namespace boost;
```

Then, we define the application's main() entry point function, which contains all the functionalities of the application:

```
int main()
{
  std::string raw_ip_address = "127.0.0.1";
  unsigned short port_num = 3333;

  try {
    asio::ip::tcp::endpoint
      ep(asio::ip::address::from_string(raw_ip_address),
      port_num);

    asio::io_service ios;

    std::shared_ptr<asio::ip::tcp::socket> sock(
      new asio::ip::tcp::socket(ios, ep.protocol()));

    sock->async_connect(ep,
      [sock](const boost::system::error_code& ec)
    {
```

```
        // If asynchronous operation has been
        // cancelled or an error occured during
        // execution, ec contains corresponding
        // error code.
        if (ec != 0) {
          if (ec == asio::error::operation_aborted) {
            std::cout << "Operation cancelled!";
          }
          else {
            std::cout << "Error occured!"
              << " Error code = "
              << ec.value()
              << ". Message: "
              << ec.message();
          }

          return;
        }
        // At this point the socket is connected and
        // can be used for communication with
        // remote application.
    });

    // Starting a thread, which will be used
    // to call the callback when asynchronous
    // operation completes.
    std::thread worker_thread([&ios](){
      try {
        ios.run();
      }
      catch (system::system_error &e) {
        std::cout << "Error occured!"
        << " Error code = " << e.code()
        << ". Message: " << e.what();
      }
    });

    // Emulating delay.
    std::this_thread::sleep_for(std::chrono::seconds(2));

    // Cancelling the initiated operation.
    sock->cancel();
```

```
      // Waiting for the worker thread to complete.
      worker_thread.join();
    }
    catch (system::system_error &e) {
      std::cout << "Error occured! Error code = " << e.code()
        << ". Message: " << e.what();

      return e.code().value();
    }

    return 0;
  }
```

How it works...

Now, let's analyze how the application works.

Our sample client application consists of a single function, which is the application's `main()` entry point function. This function begins with allocating and opening a TCP socket according to step 2 of the algorithm.

Next, the asynchronous connection operation is initiated on the socket. The callback provided to the method is implemented as a lambda function. This corresponds to steps 3 and 4 of the algorithm. Note how the fact that the operation was canceled is determined in the callback function. When an asynchronous operation is canceled, the callback is invoked and its argument that specifies the error code contains an OS dependent error code defined in Boost.Asio as `asio::error::operation_aborted`.

Then, we spawn a thread named `worker_thread`, which will be used to run the Boost.Asio event loop. In the context of this thread, the callback function will be invoked by the library. The entry point function of the `worker_thread` thread is quite simple. It contains a `try-catch` block and a call to the `asio::io_service` object's `run()` method. This corresponds to step 5 of the algorithm.

After the worker thread is spawned, the main thread is put to sleep for 2 seconds. This is to allow the connection operation to progress a bit and emulate what could be a delay between the two commands issued by the user in the real application; for example, a web browser.

According to the last step 6 of the algorithm, we call the socket object's `cancel()` method to cancel the initiated connection operation. At this point, if the operation has not yet finished, it will be canceled and the corresponding callback will be invoked with an argument that specifies the error code containing the `asio::error::operation_aborted` value to notify that the operation was canceled. However, if the operation has already finished, calling the `cancel()` method has no effect.

When the callback function returns, the worker thread exits the event loop because there are no more outstanding asynchronous operations to be executed. As a result, the thread exits its entry point function. This leads to the main thread running to its completion as well. Eventually, the application exits.

There's more...

In the previous sample, we considered the canceling of an asynchronous connection operation associated with an active TCP socket. However, any operation associated with both the TCP and UDP sockets can be canceled in a similar way. The `cancel()` method should be called on the corresponding socket object after the operation has been initiated.

In addition to this, the `async_resolve()` method of the `asio::ip::tcp::resolver` or `asio::ip::udp::resolver` class used to asynchronously resolve a DNS name can be canceled by calling the resolver object's `cancel()` method.

All asynchronous operations initiated by the corresponding free functions provided by Boost. Asio can be canceled as well by calling the `cancel()` method on an object that was passed to the free function as the first argument. This object can represent either a socket (active or passive) or a resolver.

See also

  ▸ The *Implementing an asynchronous TCP client* recipe in *Chapter 3, Implementing Client Applications*, demonstrates how to construct a more complex client application that supports the asynchronous operation cancelation functionality

  ▸ *Chapter 1, The Basics*, contains recipes that demonstrate how to synchronously connect a socket and resolve a DNS name

Shutting down and closing a socket

In some distributed applications that communicate over the TCP protocol, there is a need to transfer messages that do not have a fixed size and specific byte sequence, marking its boundary. This means that the receiving side, while reading the message from the socket, cannot determine where the message ends by analyzing the message itself with either its size or its content.

One approach to solve this problem is to structure each message in such a way that it consists of a logical header section and a logical body section. The header section has a fixed size and structure and specifies the size of the body section. This allows the receiving side to first read and parse the header, find out the size of the message body, and then properly read the rest of the message.

This approach is quite simple and is widely used. However, it brings some redundancy and additional computation overhead, which may be unacceptable in some circumstances.

Another approach can be applied when an application uses a separate socket for each message sent to its peer, which is a quite popular practice. The idea of this approach is to **shut down** the send part of the socket by the message sender after the message is written to the socket. This results in a special service message being sent to the receiver, informing the receiver that the message is over and the sender will not send anything else using the current connection.

The second approach provides many more benefits than the first one and, because it is part of the TCP protocol software, it is readily available to the developer for usage.

Another operation on a socket, that is, **closing** may seem similar to shutting down, but it is actually very different from it. Closing a socket assumes returning the socket and all the other resources associated with it back to the operating system. Just like memory, a process or a thread, a file handle or a mutex, a socket is a resource of an operating system. And like any other resource, a socket should be returned back to the operating system after it has been allocated, used, and is not needed by the application anymore. Otherwise, a resource leak may occur, which may eventually lead to the exhaustion of the resource and to the application's fault or instability of the whole operating system.

Serious issues that may occur when sockets are not closed make closing a very important operation.

The main difference between shutting down and closing a TCP socket is that closing interrupts the connection if one is established and, eventually, deallocates the socket and returns it back to the operating system, while shutting down only disables writing, reading, or both the operations on the socket and sends a service message to the peer application notifying about this fact. Shutting down a socket never results in deallocating the socket.

In this recipe, we'll see how to shut down and close a TCP socket.

How to do it...

Here, we'll consider a distributed application that consists of two parts: a client and a server to better understand how a socket shut down operation can be used to make an application layer protocol more efficient and clear when the communication between parts of distributed applications is based on binary messages of random sizes.

For simplicity, all operations in both the client and server applications are synchronous.

The client application

The purpose of the client application is to allocate the socket and connect it to the server application. After the connection is established, the application should prepare and send a request message notifying its boundary by shutting down the socket after writing the message to it.

After the request is sent, the client application should read the response. The size of the response is unknown; therefore, the reading should be performed until the server closes its socket to notify the response boundary.

We begin the client application by specifying the `include` and `using` directives:

```
#include <boost/asio.hpp>
#include <iostream>

using namespace boost;
```

Next, we define a function that accepts a reference to the socket object connected to the server and performs the communication with the server using this socket. Let's name this function `communicate()`:

```
void communicate(asio::ip::tcp::socket& sock) {
  // Allocating and filling the buffer with
  // binary data.
  const char request_buf[] = {0x48, 0x65, 0x0, 0x6c, 0x6c,
0x6f};

  // Sending the request data.
  asio::write(sock, asio::buffer(request_buf));

  // Shutting down the socket to let the
  // server know that we've sent the whole
  // request.
  sock.shutdown(asio::socket_base::shutdown_send);

  // We use extensible buffer for response
  // because we don't know the size of the
  // response message.
  asio::streambuf response_buf;

  system::error_code ec;
  asio::read(sock, response_buf, ec);
```

```
    if (ec == asio::error::eof) {
      // Whole response message has been received.
      // Here we can handle it.
    }
    else {
      throw system::system_error(ec);
    }
  }
}
```

Finally, we define an application's `main()` entry point function. This function allocates and connects the socket, and then calls the `communicate()` function defined in the previous step:

```
int main()
{
  std::string raw_ip_address = "127.0.0.1";
  unsigned short port_num = 3333;

  try {
    asio::ip::tcp::endpoint
      ep(asio::ip::address::from_string(raw_ip_address),
      port_num);

    asio::io_service ios;

    asio::ip::tcp::socket sock(ios, ep.protocol());

    sock.connect(ep);

    communicate(sock);
  }
  catch (system::system_error &e) {
    std::cout << "Error occured! Error code = " << e.code()
      << ". Message: " << e.what();

    return e.code().value();
  }

  return 0;
}
```

The server application

The server application is intended to allocate an acceptor socket and passively wait for a connection request. When the connection request arrives, it should accept it and read the data from the socket connected to the client until the client application shuts down the socket on its side. Having received the request message, the server application should send the response message notifying its boundary by shutting down the socket.

We begin the client application by specifying `include` and `using` directives:

```cpp
#include <boost/asio.hpp>
#include <iostream>

using namespace boost;
```

Next, we define a function that accepts a reference to the socket object connected to the client application and performs the communication with the client using this socket. Let's name this function `processRequest()`:

```cpp
void processRequest(asio::ip::tcp::socket& sock) {
  // We use extensible buffer because we don't
  // know the size of the request message.
  asio::streambuf request_buf;

  system::error_code ec;

  // Receiving the request.
  asio::read(sock, request_buf, ec);

  if (ec != asio::error::eof)
    throw system::system_error(ec);

  // Request received. Sending response.
  // Allocating and filling the buffer with
  // binary data.
  const char response_buf[] = { 0x48, 0x69, 0x21 };

  // Sending the request data.
  asio::write(sock, asio::buffer(response_buf));

  // Shutting down the socket to let the
  // client know that we've sent the whole
  // response.
  sock.shutdown(asio::socket_base::shutdown_send);
}
```

Finally, we define the application's `main()` entry point function. This function allocates an acceptor socket and waits for the incoming connection requests. When the connection request arrives, it obtains an active socket that is connected to the client application and calls the `processRequest()` function defined in the previous step by passing a connected socket object to it:

```cpp
int main()
{
  unsigned short port_num = 3333;

  try {
    asio::ip::tcp::endpoint ep(asio::ip::address_v4::any(),
      port_num);

    asio::io_service ios;

    asio::ip::tcp::acceptor acceptor(ios, ep);

    asio::ip::tcp::socket sock(ios);

    acceptor.accept(sock);

    processRequest(sock);
  }
  catch (system::system_error &e) {
    std::cout << "Error occured! Error code = " << e.code()
      << ". Message: " << e.what();

    return e.code().value();
  }

  return 0;
}
```

Closing a socket

In order to close an allocated socket, the `close()` method should be called on the corresponding object of the `asio::ip::tcp::socket` class. However, usually, there is no need to do it explicitly because the destructor of the socket object closes the socket if one was not closed explicitly.

How it works...

The server application is first started. In its `main()` entry point function, an acceptor socket is allocated, opened, bound to port `3333`, and starts waiting for the incoming connection request from the client.

Then, the client application is started. In its `main()` entry point function, an active socket is allocated, opened, and connected to the server. After the connection is established, the `communicate()` function is called. In this function, all the interesting things take place.

The client application writes a request message to the socket and then calls the socket's `shutdown()` method, passing an `asio::socket_base::shutdown_send` constant as an argument. This call shuts down the send part of the socket. At this point, writing to the socket is disabled, and there is no way to restore the socket state to make it writable again:

```
sock.shutdown(asio::socket_base::shutdown_send);
```

Shutting down the socket in the client application is seen in the server application as a protocol service message that arrives to the server, notifying the fact that the peer application has shut down the socket. Boost.Asio delivers this message to the application code by means of an error code returned by the `asio::read()` function. The Boost.Asio library defines this code as `asio::error::eof`. The server application uses this error code to find out when the client finishes sending the request message.

When the server application receives a full request message, the server and client exchange their roles. Now, the server writes the data, namely, the response message to the socket on its side, and the client application reads this message on its side. When the server finishes writing the response message to the socket, it shuts down the send part of its socket to imply that the whole message has been sent to its peer.

Meanwhile, the client application is blocked in the `asio::read()` function and reads the response sent by the server until the function returns with the error code equal to `asio::error::eof`, which implies that the server has finished sending the response message. When the `asio::read()` function returns with this error code, the client *knows* that it has read the whole response message, and it can then start processing it:

```
system::error_code ec;
asio::read(sock, response_buf, ec);

if (ec == asio::error::eof) {
  // Whole response message has been received.
  // Here we can handle it.
}
```

Note that after the client has shut down its socket's send part, it can still read data from the socket because the receive part of the socket stays open independently from the send part.

See also

- ► The *Writing to a TCP socket synchronously* recipe demonstrates how to write data to a TCP socket synchronously

- ► The *Reading from a TCP socket synchronously* recipe demonstrates how to read data from a TCP socket synchronously

- ► The *Implementing the HTTP client application* and *Implementing the HTTP server application* recipes in *Chapter 5, HTTP and SSL/TLS*, demonstrate how a socket shut down is used in the implementation of the HTTP protocol

3

Implementing Client Applications

In this chapter, we will cover the following topics:

- ▶ Implementing a synchronous TCP client
- ▶ Implementing a synchronous UDP client
- ▶ Implementing an asynchronous TCP client

Introduction

A **client** is a part of a distributed application that communicates with another part of this application called a **server**, in order to consume services it provides. The server, on the other hand, is a part of distributed application that passively waits for requests arriving from clients. When a request arrives, the server performs the requested operation and sends a response—the result of the operation—back to the client.

The key characteristic of a client is that it needs a service provided by the server and it initiates the communication session with that server in order to consume the service. The key characteristic of the server is that it serves the requests coming from the clients by providing a requested service.

We'll consider servers in the next chapter. In this chapter, we are going to focus on client applications and will consider several types of them in detail.

The classification of client applications

Client applications can be classified by the transport layer protocol they use for communication with the server. If the client uses a UDP protocol, it is called a **UDP client**. If it uses a TCP protocol, it is called a **TCP client** correspondingly. Of course, there are many other transport layer protocols that client applications may use for communication. Moreover, there are multiprotocol clients that can communicate over several protocols. However, they are beyond the scope of this book. In this chapter, we are going to focus on pure UDP and TCP clients as such, which are the most popular and are the most often used in general purpose software today.

The decision as to which transport layer protocol to choose for communication between the parts of a distributed application should be made at the early stages of the application design based on the application specification. Because TCP and UDP protocols are conceptually different, it may be quite difficult to switch from one of them to another at the later stages of the application development process.

Another way to classify client applications is according to whether the client is synchronous or asynchronous. A **synchronous client application** uses synchronous socket API calls that block the thread of execution until the requested operation is completed, or an error occurs. Thus, a typical synchronous TCP client would use the `asio::ip::tcp::socket::write_some()` method or the `asio::write()` free function to send a request to the sever and then use the `asio::ip::tcp::socket::read_some()` method or the `asio::read()` free function to receive a response. These methods and functions are blocking, which makes the client synchronous.

An **asynchronous client application** as opposed to a synchronous one uses asynchronous socket API calls. For example, an asynchronous TCP client may use the `asio::ip::tcp::socket::async_write_some()` method or the `asio::async_write()` free function to send a request to the server and then use the `asio::ip::tcp::socket::async_read_some()` method or the `asio::async_read()` free function to asynchronously receive a response.

Because the structure of a synchronous client significantly differs from that of an asynchronous one, the decision as to which approach to apply should be made early at the application design stage, and this decision should be based on the careful analysis of the application requirements. Besides, possible application evolution paths and new requirements that may appear in the future should be considered and taken into account.

Synchronous versus asynchronous

As usually, each approach has its advantages and disadvantages. When a synchronous approach gives better results in one situation, it may be absolutely unacceptable in another. In the latter case, an asynchronous approach should be used. Let's compare two approaches to better understand when it is more beneficial to use each of them.

The main advantage of a synchronous approach is its *simplicity*. A synchronous client is significantly easier to develop, debug, and support than a functionally equal asynchronous one. Asynchronous clients are more complex due to the fact that asynchronous operations that are used by them complete in other places in code (mainly in callbacks) than they are initiated. Usually, this requires allocating additional data structures in the free memory to keep the context of the request and callback functions, and also involves thread synchronization and other extras that may make the application structure quite complex and error-prone. Most of these extras are not required in synchronous clients. Besides, the asynchronous approach brings in additional computational and memory overhead, which makes it less efficient than a synchronous one in some conditions.

However, the synchronous approach has some functional limitations, which often make this approach unacceptable. These limitations consist of the inability to cancel a synchronous operation after it has started, or to assign it a timeout so that it gets interrupted if it is running longer than a certain amount of time. As opposed to synchronous operations, asynchronous ones can be canceled at any moment after operation initiation and before the moment it completes.

Imagine a typical modern web browser. A request cancellation is a very important feature of a client application of this kind. After issuing a command to load a particular website, the user may change his or her mind and decide to cancel the command before the page gets loaded. From the user's perspective, it would be quite strange not to be able to cancel the command until the page gets fully loaded. Therefore, this is when a synchronous approach is not a good option.

Besides the difference in the complexity and functionality described above, the two approaches differ in efficiency when it comes to running several requests in parallel.

Imagine that we are developing a web crawler, an application that traverses the pages of websites and processes them in order to extract some interesting information. Given a file with a long list of websites (say several millions), the application should traverse all the pages of each of the sites listed in the file and then process each page. Naturally, one of the key requirements of the application is to perform the task as fast as possible. Provided with these requirements, which approach should we choose, synchronous or asynchronous?

Before we answer this question, let's consider the stages of a request life cycle and their timings from the client application's perspective. Conceptually, the request life cycle consists of five stages as follows:

1. **Preparing the request**: This stage involves any operations required to prepare a request message. The duration of this step depends on the particular problem the application solves. In our example, this could be reading the next website address from the input file and constructing a string representing a request in accordance with an HTTP protocol.

2. **Transmitting a request from the client to the server**: This stage assumes the transmission of the request data from the client to the server over the network. The duration of this step does not depend on a client application. It depends on the properties and the current state of the network.

3. **Processing the request by the server**: The duration of this step depends on the server's properties and its current load. In our example, the server application is a web server and the request processing lies in constructing a requested web page, which may involve I/O operations such as reading files and loading data from a database.

4. **Transmitting a response from the server to the client**: Like stage 2, this stage also assumes the transmission of the data over the network; however, this time it is in the opposite direction—from the server to the client. The duration of this stage does not depend on the client or the server. It only depends on the properties and the state of the network.

5. **Processing the response by the client**: The duration of this stage depends on a particular task that the client application is intended to perform. In our example, this could be scanning the web page, extracting interesting information and storing it into a database.

Note that, for the sake of simplicity, we omitted low-level substages such as connection establishment and connection shutdown, which are important when using TCP protocol but don't add a substantial value in our conceptual model of a request life cycle.

As we can see, only in stages 1 and 5 does the client perform some effective job related to the request. Having initiated the transmission of the request data at the end of stage 1, the client has to wait during the next three stages (2, 3, and 4) of the request life cycle before it can receive the response and process it.

Now, with the stages of the request life cycle in mind, let's see what happens when we apply synchronous and asynchronous approaches to implement our sample web crawler.

If we apply a synchronous approach, the thread of execution processing a single request synchronously will be sleeping during stages 2-4 of the request life cycle, and only during stages 1 and 5, will it perform an effective job (for simplicity, we assume that stages 1 and 5 don't include instructions that block the thread). This means that the resource of an operating system, namely a thread, is used inefficiently, because there are number of times when it is simply doing nothing while there is still a lot of work available—millions of other pages to request and process. In this situation, an asynchronous approach seems to be more efficient. With an asynchronous approach, instead of a thread being blocked during stages 2-4 of a request life cycle, it can be effectively used to perform stages 1 or 5 of another request.

Thus, we direct a single thread to process the different stages of different requests (this is called **overlapping**), which results in the more efficient usage of a thread and consequently increases the overall performance of the application.

However, an asynchronous approach is not always more efficient than a synchronous one. As it has been mentioned, asynchronous operations imply additional computational overheads, which means that the overall duration of an asynchronous operation (from initiation till completion) is somewhat bigger than the equivalent synchronous one. This means that, if the average total duration of stages 2-4 is less than the overhead of the timing asynchronous approach per single request, then a synchronous approach turns out to be more efficient, and therefore may be considered to be the right way to go.

Assessing the total duration of stages 2-4 of the request life cycle and the overhead of the asynchronous approach is usually done experimentally. The duration may significantly vary, and it depends on the properties and the state of the network through which the requests and responses are transmitted and also on the properties and the load level of the server application that serves the request.

The sample protocol

In this chapter, we are going to consider three recipes, each of which demonstrates how to implement a particular type of a client application: the synchronous UDP client, synchronous TCP client, and asynchronous TCP client. In all the recipes, it is assumed that the client application communicates with the server application using the following simple application-level protocol.

The server application accepts a request represented as an ASCII string. The string has the following format:

```
EMULATE_LONG_COMP_OP [s]<LF>
```

Where [s] is a positive integer value and <LF> is ASCII a new-line symbol.

The server interprets this string as a request to perform a dummy operation that lasts for [s] seconds. For example, a request string may look as follows:

```
"EMULATE_LONG_COMP_OP 10\n"
```

This means that the client sending this request wants the server to perform the dummy operation for 10 seconds and then send a response to it.

Like the request, the response returned by the server is represented by an ASCII string. It may either be OK<LF> if the operation completes successfully or ERROR<LF> if the operation fails.

Implementing a synchronous TCP client

A synchronous TCP client is a part of a distributed application that complies with the following statements:

> ▸ Acts as a client in the client-server communication model
>
> ▸ Communicates with the server application using a TCP protocol
>
> ▸ Uses I/O and control operations (at least those I/O operations that are related to communication with a server) that block the thread of execution until the corresponding operation completes, or an error occurs

A typical synchronous TCP client works according to the following algorithm:

1. Obtain the IP-address and the protocol port number of the server application.
2. Allocate an active socket.
3. Establish a connection with the server application.
4. Exchange messages with the server.
5. Shut down the connection.
6. Deallocate the socket.

This recipe demonstrates how to implement a synchronous TCP client application with Boost.Asio.

How to do it...

The following code sample demonstrates a possible implementation of a synchronous TCP client application with Boost.Asio. The client uses the application layer protocol described in the introduction section of this chapter:

```
#include <boost/asio.hpp>
#include <iostream>

using namespace boost;
```

```
class SyncTCPClient {
public:
  SyncTCPClient(const std::string& raw_ip_address,
    unsigned short port_num) :
    m_ep(asio::ip::address::from_string(raw_ip_address),
    port_num),
    m_sock(m_ios) {

    m_sock.open(m_ep.protocol());
  }

  void connect() {
    m_sock.connect(m_ep);
  }

  void close() {
    m_sock.shutdown(
      boost::asio::ip::tcp::socket::shutdown_both);
    m_sock.close();
  }

  std::string emulateLongComputationOp(
    unsigned int duration_sec) {

    std::string request = "EMULATE_LONG_COMP_OP "
      + std::to_string(duration_sec)
      + "\n";

    sendRequest(request);
    return receiveResponse();
  };

private:
  void sendRequest(const std::string& request) {
    asio::write(m_sock, asio::buffer(request));
  }

  std::string receiveResponse() {
    asio::streambuf buf;
    asio::read_until(m_sock, buf, '\n');
```

```
      std::istream input(&buf);

      std::string response;
      std::getline(input, response);

      return response;
  }

private:
  asio::io_service m_ios;

  asio::ip::tcp::endpoint m_ep;
  asio::ip::tcp::socket m_sock;
};

int main()
{
  const std::string raw_ip_address = "127.0.0.1";
  const unsigned short port_num = 3333;

  try {
    SyncTCPClient client(raw_ip_address, port_num);

    // Sync connect.
    client.connect();

    std::cout << "Sending request to the server... "
      << std::endl;

    std::string response =
      client.emulateLongComputationOp(10);

    std::cout << "Response received: " << response
      << std::endl;

    // Close the connection and free resources.
    client.close();
  }
  catch (system::system_error &e) {
    std::cout << "Error occured! Error code = " << e.code()
      << ". Message: " << e.what();
```

```
        return e.code().value();
    }

    return 0;
}
```

How it works...

The sample client application consists of two main components—the `SyncTCPClient` class and the application entry point function `main()` in which the `SyncTCPClient` class is used to communicate with the server application. Let's consider each component separately.

The SyncTCPClient class

The `SyncTCPClient` class is the key component in the sample. It implements and provides access to the communication functionality.

The class has three private members as follows:

- ▸ `asio::io_service m_ios`: This is the object providing access to the operating system's communication services, which are used by the socket object

- ▸ `asio::ip::tcp::endpoint m_ep`: This is an endpoint designating the server application

- ▸ `asio::ip::tcp::socket m_sock`: This is the socket used for communication

Each object of the class is intended to communicate with a single server application; therefore, the class's constructor accepts the server IP-address and the protocol port number as its arguments. These values are used to instantiate the `m_ep` object in the constructor's initialization list. The socket object `m_sock` is instantiated and opened in the constructor too.

The three public methods comprise the interface of the `SyncTCPClient` class. The first method named `connect()` is quite simple; it performs the connection of the socket to the server. The `close()` method shuts the connection down and closes the socket, which leads to the operating system's socket and other resources associated with it to be deallocated.

The third interface method is `emulateLongComputationOp(unsigned int duration_sec)`. This method is where the I/O operations are performed. It begins with preparing the request string according to the protocol. Then, the request is passed to the class's private method `sendRequest(const std::string& request)`, which sends it to the server. When the request is sent and the `sendRequest()` method returns, the `receiveResponse()` method is called to receive the response from the server. When the response is received, the `receiveResponse()` method returns the string containing the response. After this, the `emulateLongComputationOp()` method returns the response to its caller.

Let's look at the `sendRequest()` and `receiveResponse()` methods in more detail.

The `sendRequest()` method has the following prototype:

```
void sendRequest(const std::string& request)
```

Its purpose is to send a string, passed to it as an argument, to the server. In order to send the data to the server, the `asio::write()` free synchronous function is used. The function returns when the request is sent. That's it about the `sendRequest()` method. Basically, all it does is, it fully delegates its job to the `asio::write()` free function.

Having sent the request, now we want to receive the response from the server. This is the purpose of the `receiveResponse()` method of the `SyncTCPClient` class. To perform its job, method uses the `asio::read_until()` free function. According to the application layer protocol, the response message sent by the server may vary in length, but must end with the \n symbol; therefore, we specify this symbol as a delimiter when calling the function:

```
asio::streambuf buf;
asio::read_until(m_sock, buf, '\n');
```

The function blocks the thread of execution until it encounters the \n symbol as a part of the message that arrived from the server. When the function returns, the stream buffer `buf` contains the response. The data is then copied from the `buf` buffer to the `response` string and the latter is returned to the caller. The `emulateLongComputationOp()` method in turn returns the response to its caller—the `main()` function.

One thing to note with regard to the `SyncTCPClient` class is that it contains no error handling-related code. That's because the class uses only those overloads of Boost.Asio functions and objects' methods that throw exceptions in case of failure. It is assumed that the user of the class is responsible for catching and handling the exceptions.

The main() entry point function

This function acts as a user of the `SyncTCPClient` class. Having obtained the server IP-address and the protocol port number (this part is omitted from the sample), it instantiates and uses an object of the `SyncTCPClient` class to communicate with the server in order to consume its service, mainly to emulate an operation on the server that performs dummy calculations for 10 seconds. The code of this function is simple and self-explanatory and thus requires no additional comments.

See also

> ▸ *Chapter 2, I/O Operations*, includes recipes providing detailed discussions on how to perform synchronous I/O

Implementing a synchronous UDP client

A synchronous UDP client is a part of a distributed application that complies with the following statements:

- Acts as a client in the client-server communication model
- Communicates with the server application using UDP protocol
- Uses I/O and control operations (at least those I/O operations that are related to communication with the server) that block the thread of execution until the corresponding operation completes, or an error occurs

A typical synchronous UDP client works according to the following algorithm:

1. Obtain an IP-address and a protocol port number of each server the client application is intended to communicate with.
2. Allocate a UDP socket.
3. Exchange messages with the servers.
4. Deallocate the socket.

This recipe demonstrates how to implement a synchronous UDP client application with Boost.Asio.

How to do it...

The following code sample demonstrates a possible implementation of a synchronous UDP client application with Boost.Asio. It is assumed that the client uses UDP protocol with the underlying IPv4 protocol for communication:

```
#include <boost/asio.hpp>
#include <iostream>

using namespace boost;

class SyncUDPClient {
public:
  SyncUDPClient() :
    m_sock(m_ios) {

    m_sock.open(asio::ip::udp::v4());
  }
```

```cpp
    std::string emulateLongComputationOp(
      unsigned int duration_sec,
      const std::string& raw_ip_address,
      unsigned short port_num) {

      std::string request = "EMULATE_LONG_COMP_OP "
        + std::to_string(duration_sec)
        + "\n";

      asio::ip::udp::endpoint ep(
        asio::ip::address::from_string(raw_ip_address),
        port_num);

      sendRequest(ep, request);
      return receiveResponse(ep);
    };

private:
  void sendRequest(const asio::ip::udp::endpoint& ep,
    const std::string& request) {

    m_sock.send_to(asio::buffer(request), ep);
  }

  std::string receiveResponse(asio::ip::udp::endpoint& ep) {
    char response[6];
    std::size_t bytes_recieved =
      m_sock.receive_from(asio::buffer(response), ep);

    m_sock.shutdown(asio::ip::udp::socket::shutdown_both);
    return std::string(response, bytes_recieved);
  }

private:
  asio::io_service m_ios;

  asio::ip::udp::socket m_sock;
};

int main()
{
```

```
const std::string server1_raw_ip_address = "127.0.0.1";
const unsigned short server1_port_num = 3333;

const std::string server2_raw_ip_address = "192.168.1.10";
const unsigned short server2_port_num = 3334;

try {
  SyncUDPClient client;

  std::cout << "Sending request to the server #1 ... "
    << std::endl;

  std::string response =
    client.emulateLongComputationOp(10,
    server1_raw_ip_address, server1_port_num);

  std::cout << "Response from the server #1 received: "
    << response << std::endl;

  std::cout << "Sending request to the server #2... "
    << std::endl;

  response =
    client.emulateLongComputationOp(10,
    server2_raw_ip_address, server2_port_num);

  std::cout << "Response from the server #2 received: "
    << response << std::endl;
}
catch (system::system_error &e) {
  std::cout << "Error occured! Error code = " << e.code()
    << ". Message: " << e.what();

  return e.code().value();
}

return 0;
}
```

How it works...

The sample consists of two main components—the `SyncUDPClient` class and the application entry point function `main()` that uses the `SyncUDPClient` class to communicate with two server applications. Let's consider each component separately.

The SyncUDPClient class

The `SyncUDPClient` class is the key component in the sample. It implements the server communication functionality and provides access to it for the user.

The class has two private members as follows:

▸ `asio::io_service m_ios`: This is the object providing access to the operating system's communication services, which are used by the socket object

▸ `asio::ip::udp::socket m_sock`: This is the UDP socket used for communication

The socket object `m_sock` is instantiated and opened in the class's constructor. Because the client is intended to use IPv4 protocol, we pass the object returned by the `asio::ip::udp::v4()` static method to the socket's `open()` method to designate the socket to use IPv4 protocol.

Because the `SyncUDPClient` class implements communication over UDP protocol, which is a connectionless protocol, a single object of this class can be used to communicate with multiple servers. The interface of the class consists of a single method—`emulateLongComputationOp()`. This method can be used to communicate with the server just after the object of the `SyncUDPClient` class is instantiated. The following is the prototype of the method:

```
std::string emulateLongComputationOp(
        unsigned int duration_sec,
        const std::string& raw_ip_address,
        unsigned short port_num)
```

Besides the `duration_sec` argument that represents a request parameter, the method accepts the server IP-address and the protocol port number. This method may be called multiple times to communicate with different servers.

The method begins with preparing a request string according to the application layer protocol and creating an endpoint object designating the target server application. Then, the request string and the endpoint object are passed to the class's private method `sendRequest()`, which sends the request message to the specified server. When the request is sent and the `sendRequest()` method returns, the `receiveResponse()` method is called to receive a response from the server.

When the response is received, the `receiveResponse()` method returns the string containing the response. In turn, the `emulateLongComputationOp()` method returns the response to its caller. The `sendRequest()` method uses the socket object's `send_to()` method to send the request message to a particular server. Let's have a look at the declaration of this method:

```
template <typename ConstBufferSequence>
std::size_t send_to(const ConstBufferSequence& buffers,
    const endpoint_type& destination)
```

The method accepts a buffer containing the request and an endpoint designating the server to which the content of the buffer should be sent as arguments and blocks until the whole buffer is sent, or an error occurs. Note that, if the method returns without an error, it only means that the request has been sent and *does not* mean that the request has been received by the server. UDP protocol doesn't guarantee message delivery and it provides no means to check whether the datagram has been successfully received on the server-side or got lost somewhere on its way to the server.

Having sent the request, now we want to receive the response from the server. This is the purpose of the `receiveResponse()` method of the `SyncUDPClient` class. This method begins with allocating a buffer that will hold the response message. We choose the size of the buffer such that it can fit the largest message that the server may send according to the application layer protocol. This message is an `ERROR\n` string that consists of six ASCII symbols, which is therefore 6 bytes long; hence is the size of our buffer - 6 bytes. Because the buffer is small enough, we allocate it on the stack.

To read the response data arriving from the server, we use the socket object's `receive_from()` method. Here is the prototype of the method:

```
template <typename MutableBufferSequence>
std::size_t receive_from(const MutableBufferSequence& buffers,
    endpoint_type& sender_endpoint)
```

This method copies a datagram that came from the server designated by the `sender_endpoint` object to the buffer specified by the `buffers` argument.

There are two things to note about socket object's `receive_from()` method. The first thing is that this method is synchronous and it blocks the thread of execution until the datagram arrives from the specified server. If the datagram never arrives (for example, gets lost somewhere on its way to the client), the method will never unblock and the whole application will hang. The second thing is that if the size of the datagram that arrives from the server is larger than the size of the supplied buffer, the method will fail.

After the response is received, the `std::string` object is created, initialized with a response string, and returned to the caller—the `emulateLongComputationOp()` method. This in turn returns the response to its caller—the `main()` function.

The `SyncUDPClient` class does not contain error handling-related code. That's is because it uses only those overloads of Boost.Asio functions and objects' methods that throw exceptions in case of failure. It is assumed that the user of the class is responsible for catching and handling the exceptions.

The main() entry point function

In this function, we use the `SyncUDPClient` class in order to communicate with two server applications. Firstly, we obtain the IP-addresses and the port numbers of the target server applications. Then, we instantiate the object of the `SyncUDPClient` class and call the object's `emulateLongComputationOp()` method twice to synchronously consume the same service from two different servers.

See also

> ▸ *Chapter 2, I/O Operations*, includes recipes that provide detailed discussions on how to perform synchronous I/O

Implementing an asynchronous TCP client

As it has already been mentioned in the introduction section of this chapter, the simplest asynchronous client is structurally more complex than equivalent synchronous one. When we add a feature such as request canceling to the asynchronous client, it becomes even more complex.

In this recipe, we'll consider an asynchronous TCP client application supporting the asynchronous execution of the requests and request canceling functionality. Here is the list of requirements the application will fulfill:

> ▸ Input from the user should be processed in a separate thread—the user interface thread. This thread should never be blocked for a noticeable amount of time.

> ▸ The user should be able to issue multiple requests to different servers.

> ▸ The user should be able to issue a new request before the previously issued requests complete.

> ▸ The user should be able to cancel the previously issued requests before they complete.

How to do it...

As our application needs to support request canceling, we begin with specifying settings that enable request canceling on Windows:

```
#include <boost/predef.h> // Tools to identify the OS.

// We need this to enable cancelling of I/O operations on
// Windows XP, Windows Server 2003 and earlier.
// Refer to "http://www.boost.org/doc/libs/1_58_0/
// doc/html/boost_asio/reference/basic_stream_socket/
// cancel/overload1.html" for details.
#ifdef BOOST_OS_WINDOWS
#define _WIN32_WINNT 0x0501

#if _WIN32_WINNT <= 0x0502 // Windows Server 2003 or earlier.
  #define BOOST_ASIO_DISABLE_IOCP
  #define BOOST_ASIO_ENABLE_CANCELIO
#endif
#endif
```

Then, we include the necessary headers and specify the `using` directive for our convenience:

```
#include <boost/asio.hpp>

#include <thread>
#include <mutex>
#include <memory>
#include <iostream>


using namespace boost;
```

We continue with defining a data type representing a pointer to a callback function. Because our client application is going to be asynchronous, we need a notion of callback as a request completion notification mechanism. Later, it will become clear as to why we need it and how it is used:

```
// Function pointer type that points to the callback
// function which is called when a request is complete.
typedef void(*Callback) (unsigned int request_id,
  const std::string& response,
  const system::error_code& ec);
```

Next, we define a data structure whose purpose is to keep the data related to a particular request while it is being executed. Let's name it `Session`:

```cpp
// Structure represents a context of a single request.
struct Session {
  Session(asio::io_service& ios,
  const std::string& raw_ip_address,
  unsigned short port_num,
  const std::string& request,
  unsigned int id,
  Callback callback) :
  m_sock(ios),
  m_ep(asio::ip::address::from_string(raw_ip_address),
  port_num),
  m_request(request),
  m_id(id),
  m_callback(callback),
  m_was_cancelled(false) {}

  asio::ip::tcp::socket m_sock; // Socket used for communication
  asio::ip::tcp::endpoint m_ep; // Remote endpoint.
  std::string m_request;        // Request string.

  // streambuf where the response will be stored.
  asio::streambuf m_response_buf;
  std::string m_response; // Response represented as a string.

  // Contains the description of an error if one occurs during
  // the request life cycle.
  system::error_code m_ec;

  unsigned int m_id; // Unique ID assigned to the request.

  // Pointer to the function to be called when the request
  // completes.
  Callback m_callback;

  bool m_was_cancelled;
  std::mutex m_cancel_guard;
};
```

The purpose of all the fields that the `Session` data structure contains will become clear later as we go.

Next, we define a class that provides the asynchronous communication functionality.
Let's name it `AsyncTCPClient`:

```cpp
class AsyncTCPClient : public boost::noncopyable {
class AsyncTCPClient : public boost::noncopyable {
public:
    AsyncTCPClient(){
        m_work.reset(new boost::asio::io_service::work(m_ios));

        m_thread.reset(new std::thread([this](){
            m_ios.run();
        }));
    }

    void emulateLongComputationOp(
        unsigned int duration_sec,
        const std::string& raw_ip_address,
        unsigned short port_num,
        Callback callback,
        unsigned int request_id) {

        // Preparing the request string.
        std::string request = "EMULATE_LONG_CALC_OP "
            + std::to_string(duration_sec)
            + "\n";

        std::shared_ptr<Session> session =
            std::shared_ptr<Session>(new Session(m_ios,
            raw_ip_address,
            port_num,
            request,
            request_id,
            callback));

        session->m_sock.open(session->m_ep.protocol());

        // Add new session to the list of active sessions so
        // that we can access it if the user decides to cancel
        // the corresponding request before it completes.
        // Because active sessions list can be accessed from
        // multiple threads, we guard it with a mutex to avoid
        // data corruption.
        std::unique_lock<std::mutex>
            lock(m_active_sessions_guard);
```

```
m_active_sessions[request_id] = session;
lock.unlock();

session->m_sock.async_connect(session->m_ep,
    [this, session](const system::error_code& ec)
    {
    if (ec != 0) {
        session->m_ec = ec;
        onRequestComplete(session);
        return;
    }

    std::unique_lock<std::mutex>
        cancel_lock(session->m_cancel_guard);

    if (session->m_was_cancelled) {
        onRequestComplete(session);
        return;
    }

        asio::async_write(session->m_sock,
                    asio::buffer(session->m_request),
    [this, session](const boost::system::error_code& ec,
                    std::size_t bytes_transferred)
    {
    if (ec != 0) {
        session->m_ec = ec;
        onRequestComplete(session);
        return;
    }

    std::unique_lock<std::mutex>
        cancel_lock(session->m_cancel_guard);

    if (session->m_was_cancelled) {
        onRequestComplete(session);
        return;
    }

        asio::async_read_until(session->m_sock,
                        session->m_response_buf,
                        '\n',
    [this, session](const boost::system::error_code& ec,
        std::size_t bytes_transferred)
```

```
            {
            if (ec != 0) {
                session->m_ec = ec;
            } else {
                std::istream strm(&session->m_response_buf);
                std::getline(strm, session->m_response);
            }

            onRequestComplete(session);
        });});});
    };

    // Cancels the request.
    void cancelRequest(unsigned int request_id) {
        std::unique_lock<std::mutex>
            lock(m_active_sessions_guard);

        auto it = m_active_sessions.find(request_id);
        if (it != m_active_sessions.end()) {
            std::unique_lock<std::mutex>
                cancel_lock(it->second->m_cancel_guard);

            it->second->m_was_cancelled = true;
            it->second->m_sock.cancel();
        }
    }

    void close() {
        // Destroy work object. This allows the I/O thread to
        // exits the event loop when there are no more pending
        // asynchronous operations.
        m_work.reset(NULL);

        // Wait for the I/O thread to exit.
        m_thread->join();
    }

private:
    void onRequestComplete(std::shared_ptr<Session> session) {
        // Shutting down the connection. This method may
        // fail in case socket is not connected. We don't care
        // about the error code if this function fails.
        boost::system::error_code ignored_ec;
```

```
        session->m_sock.shutdown(
            asio::ip::tcp::socket::shutdown_both,
            ignored_ec);

        // Remove session form the map of active sessions.
        std::unique_lock<std::mutex>
            lock(m_active_sessions_guard);

        auto it = m_active_sessions.find(session->m_id);
        if (it != m_active_sessions.end())
            m_active_sessions.erase(it);

        lock.unlock();

        boost::system::error_code ec;

        if (session->m_ec == 0 && session->m_was_cancelled)
            ec = asio::error::operation_aborted;
        else
            ec = session->m_ec;

        // Call the callback provided by the user.
        session->m_callback(session->m_id,
            session->m_response, ec);
    };

private:
    asio::io_service m_ios;
    std::map<int, std::shared_ptr<Session>> m_active_sessions;
    std::mutex m_active_sessions_guard;
    std::unique_ptr<boost::asio::io_service::work> m_work;
    std::unique_ptr<std::thread> m_thread;
};
```

This class is the key component in our sample, providing most of the functionality of the application. This functionality is accessible to the user of the class through its public interface that contains three public methods:

- ▶ void emulateLongComputationOp (unsigned int duration_sec, const std::string& raw_ip_address, unsigned short port_num, Callback callback, unsigned int request_id): This method initiates a request to the server

- ▶ void cancelRequest (unsigned int request_id): This method cancels the previously initiated request designated by the request_id argument

- ▶ void close(): This method blocks the calling thread until all the currently running requests complete and deinitializes the client. When this method returns, the corresponding instance of the AsyncTCPClient class can't be used anymore.

Now, we define a function that will serve as a callback, which we'll pass to the AsyncTCPClient::emulateLongComputationOp() method. In our case, this function is quite simple. It outputs the result of the request execution and the response message to the standard output stream if the request is completed successfully:

```
void handler(unsigned int request_id,
        const std::string& response,
            const system::error_code& ec)
{
  if (ec == 0) {
    std::cout << "Request #" << request_id
      << " has completed. Response: "
      << response << std::endl;
  } else if (ec == asio::error::operation_aborted) {
    std::cout << "Request #" << request_id
      << " has been cancelled by the user."
          << std::endl;
  } else {
    std::cout << "Request #" << request_id
      << " failed! Error code = " << ec.value()
      << ". Error message = " << ec.message()
          << std::endl;
  }

  return;
}
```

The `handler()` function's signature corresponds to the function pointer type `Callback` defined earlier.

Now that we have all the ingredients, we define an entry point of the application—the `main()` function—which demonstrates how to use the components defined above in order to communicate with the server. In our sample function, `main()` emulates the behavior of a human user by initiating three requests and canceling one of them:

```cpp
int main()
{
  try {
    AsyncTCPClient client;

    // Here we emulate the user's behavior.

    // User initiates a request with id 1.
    client.emulateLongComputationOp(10, "127.0.0.1", 3333,
       handler, 1);
    // Then does nothing for 5 seconds.
    std::this_thread::sleep_for(std::chrono::seconds(5));
    // Then initiates another request with id 2.
    client.emulateLongComputationOp(11, "127.0.0.1", 3334,
       handler, 2);
    // Then decides to cancel the request with id 1.
    client.cancelRequest(1);
    // Does nothing for another 6 seconds.
    std::this_thread::sleep_for(std::chrono::seconds(6));
    // Initiates one more request assigning ID3 to it.
    client.emulateLongComputationOp(12, "127.0.0.1", 3335,
       handler, 3);
    // Does nothing for another 15 seconds.
    std::this_thread::sleep_for(std::chrono::seconds(15));
    // Decides to exit the application.
    client.close();
  }
  catch (system::system_error &e) {
    std::cout << "Error occured! Error code = " << e.code()
       << ". Message: " << e.what();

    return e.code().value();
  }

  return 0;
};
```

How it works...

Our sample client application uses two threads of execution. The first one—UI thread—is responsible for processing a user input and initiating requests. The responsibility of the second thread—I/O thread—is to run the event loop and call the asynchronous operation's callback routines. Such configuration allows us to make our application's user interface responsive.

Starting the application – the main() entry point function

The `main()` function is invoked in the context of the UI thread. This function emulates the behavior of the user who initiates and cancels requests. Firstly, it creates an instance of the `AsyncTCPClient` class and then calls its `emulateLongComputationOp()` method three times to initiate three asynchronous requests, each time specifying a different target server. The first request (the one assigned ID 1) is canceled by calling the `cancelRequest()` method several seconds after the request has been initiated.

Request completion – the handler() callback function

For all three requests initiated in the `main()` function `handler()` is specified as a callback. This function is called when the request is finished regardless of the reason as to why it finished—be it a successful completion or an error. Also, this function is called when the request is canceled by the user. The function accepts three arguments as follows:

- ▶ `unsigned int request_id`: This contains the unique identifier of the request. This is the same identifier that was assigned to the request when it was initiated.

- ▶ `std::string& response`: This contains the response data. This value is considered valid only if the request is completed successfully and is not canceled.

- ▶ `system::error_code& ec`: If an error occurs during a request life cycle, this object contains the error information. If the request was canceled, it contains the `asio::error::operation_aborted` value.

The `handler()` function is quite simple in our sample. Based on the values of the parameters passed to it, it outputs information about the finished request.

The AsyncTCPClient class – initializing

As it has already been mentioned, all the functionality related to communication with the server application is hidden in the `AsyncTCPClient` class. This class has a nonempty constructor that accepts no arguments and does two things. Firstly, it instantiates an object of the `asio::io_service::work` class passing an instance of the `asio::io_service` class named `m_ios` to its constructor. Then, it spawns a thread that calls the `run()` method of the `m_ios` object. The object of the `asio::io_service::work` class keeps threads running event loop from exiting this loop when there are no pending asynchronous operations. The spawned thread plays the role of I/O thread in our application; in the context of this thread, the callbacks assigned asynchronous operations will be invoked.

The AsyncTCPClient class – initiating a request

The emulateLongComputationOp() method is intended to initiate an asynchronous request. It accepts five arguments. The first one named duration_sec represents the request parameter according to the application layer protocol. The raw_ip_address and port_num specify the server to which the request should be sent. The next argument is a pointer to a callback function, which will be called when the request is complete. We'll turn back to the discussion of the callback later in this section. The last argument request_id is the unique identifier of the request. This identifier is associated with the request and is used to refer to it later, for example, when there is a need to cancel it.

The emulateLongComputationOp() method begins with preparing a request string and allocating an instance of the Session structure that keeps the data associated with the request including a socket object that is used to communicate with the server.

Then, the socket is opened and the pointer to the Session object is added to the m_active_sessions map. This map contains pointers to the Session objects associated with all active requests, that is, those requests that have been initiated but have not finished yet. When the request completes, before the corresponding callback is called, the pointer to the Session object associated with this request is removed from the map.

The request_id argument is used as a key of the corresponding Session object added to the map. We need to cache the Session objects in order to have access to them in case the user decides to cancel the previously initiated request. If we would not need to support canceling of a request, we could avoid using the m_active_sessions map.

We synchronize the access to the m_active_sessions map with a m_active_session_guard mutex. Synchronization is necessary because the map can be accessed from multiple threads. Items are added to it in UI thread, and removed in an I/O thread that calls a callback when the corresponding request is finished.

Now, when the pointer to the corresponding Session object is cached, we need to connect the socket to the server, which we do by calling the socket's async_connect() method:

```
session->m_sock.async_connect(session->m_ep,
    [this, session](const system::error_code& ec)
    {
            // ...
    });
```

An endpoint object designating the server to which we want to connect and a callback function to be called when the connection is complete or an error occurs, are passed as arguments to this method. In our sample we use lambda function as a callback function. The call to the socket's async_connect() method is the last statement in the emulateLongComputationOp() method. When async_connect() returns, emulateLongComputationOp() returns too, which means that the request has been initiated.

Let's have a closer look at the lambda function that we pass to `async_connect()` as a callback. Here is its code:

```
[this, session](const system::error_code&ec)
{
  if (ec != 0) {
    session->m_ec = ec;
    onRequestComplete(session);
    return;
  }

  std::unique_lock<std::mutex>
    cancel_lock(session->m_cancel_guard);

  if (session->m_was_cancelled) {
    onRequestComplete(session);
    return;
  }

  asio::async_write(session->m_sock,
  asio::buffer(session->m_request),
        [this, session](const boost::system::error_code& ec,
              std::size_t bytes_transferred)
              {
                    //...
        });
}
```

The callback begins with checking the error code passed to it as the `ec` argument, the value of which when different from zero means that the corresponding asynchronous operation has failed. In case of failure, we store the `ec` value in the corresponding `Session` object, call the class's `onRequestComplete()` private method passing the `Session` object to it as an argument, and then return.

If the `ec` object designates success, we lock the `m_cancel_guard` mutex (the member of the request descriptor object) and check whether the request has not been canceled yet. More details about the canceling request are provided later in this section, where the `cancelRequest()` method is considered.

If we see that the request has not been canceled, we initiate the next asynchronous operation calling the Boost.Asio free function `async_write()` to send the request data to the server. Again, we pass to it a lambda function as a callback. This callback is very similar to the one passed to the `anync_connect()` method when the asynchronous connection operation was initiated. We first check the error code and then if it indicates success, we check whether or not the request has been canceled. Also, if it has not, we initiate the next asynchronous operation—`async_read_until()`—in order to receive a response from the server:

```
[this, session](const boost::system::error_code& ec,
        std::size_t bytes_transferred){
  if (ec != 0) {
    session->m_ec = ec;
    onRequestComplete(session);
    return;
  }

  std::unique_lock<std::mutex>
    cancel_lock(session->m_cancel_guard);

  if (session->m_was_cancelled) {
    onRequestComplete(session);
    return;
  }

  asio::async_read_until(session->m_sock,
      session->m_response_buf, '\n',
    [this, session](const boost::system::error_code& ec,
          std::size_t b'ytes_transferred)
      {
    // ...
      });
}
```

Again, we pass a lambda function as a callback argument to the `async_read_until()` free function. This callback function is quite simple:

```
[this, session](const boost::system::error_code& ec,
    std::size_t bytes_transferred)
{
  if (ec != 0) {
    session->m_ec = ec;
  } else {
```

```
    std::istream strm(&session->m_response_buf);
    std::getline(strm, session->m_response);
}


onRequestComplete(session);
}
```

It checks the error code and in the case of success, it stores the received response data in the corresponding `Session` object. Then, the `AsyncTCPClient` class's private method `onRequestComplete()` is called and the `Session` object is passed to it as an argument.

The `onRequestComplete()` method is called whenever the request completes with any result. It is called when the request completes successfully, when the request fails at any stage of its life cycle, or when it is canceled by the user. The purpose of this method is to perform a cleanup and then to call a callback provided by the caller of the `emulateLongComputationOp()` method, when initiating this request.

The `onRequestComplete()` method begins with shutting down the socket. Note that here we use the overload of the socket's `shutdown()` method, which doesn't throw exceptions. We don't care if the shutting down of the connection fails as this is not a critical operation in our case. Then, we remove the corresponding entry from the `m_active_sessions` map as the request is finished and hence it is not active anymore. Also, as the last step, the user supplied callback is called. After the callback function returns, the request life cycle is finished.

The AsyncTCPClient class – canceling the request

Now, let's take a look at the `cancelRequst()` method of the `AsyncTCPClient` class. This method accepts an identifier of the request to be canceled as an argument. It begins with looking for the `Session` object corresponding to the specified request in the `m_active_sessions` map. If one is found, it calls the `cancel()` method on the socket object stored in this `Session` object. This leads to the interruption of the currently running asynchronous operation associated with this socket object.

However, there is a chance that the `cancelRequest()` method will be called at the moment when one asynchronous operation has already been completed and the next one has not been initiated yet. For example, imagine that the I/O thread is now running the callback of the `async_connect()` operation associated with a particular socket. At this moment, no asynchronous operation associated with this socket is in progress (because the next asynchronous operation `async_write()` has not been initiated yet); therefore, calling `cancel()` on this socket will have no effect. That's why we use an additional flag `Session::m_was_cancelled` designating, as its name suggests, whether the request has been canceled (or to be more precise, whether the `cancelRequest()` method has been called by the user). In the callback of the asynchronous operation, we look at the value of this flag before initiating the next asynchronous operation. If we see that the flag is set (which means that the request was canceled), we don't initiate the next asynchronous operation, but instead we interrupt the request execution and call the `onRequestComplete()` method.

We use the `Session::m_cancel_guard` mutex in the `cancelRequest()` method and in the callbacks of the asynchronous operations such as `async_connect()` and `async_write()` to enforce the following order of operations: request can be canceled either before the value of the `Session::m_was_cancelled` flag is tested in the callback, or after the next asynchronous operation is initiated. This order guarantees the proper canceling of a request whenever a user calls the `cancelRequest()` method.

The AsyncTCPClient class – closing the client

After the client has been used and is not needed anymore, it should be properly closed. The `close()` method of the `AsyncTCPClient` class allows us to do that. Firstly, this method destroys the `m_work` object that allows the I/O thread to exit the event message loop when all the asynchronous operations are completed. Then, it joins the I/O thread to wait until it exits.

After the `close()` method returns, the corresponding object of the `AsyncTCPClient` class cannot be used anymore.

There's more...

The `AsyncTCPClient` class in the presented sample implements an asynchronous **single-threaded** TCP client. It uses a single thread that runs the event loop and processes the requests. Usually, when the request rate is low, the size of the response is not large and the request handler does not perform the complex and time-consuming processing of the response (stage 5 of the request life cycle); one thread is enough.

However, when we want the client to make millions of requests and process them as fast as possible, we may want to turn our client into a **multithreaded** one, where multiple threads may run several requests truly simultaneously. Of course, it assumes that the computer running the client is a multicore or a multiprocessor computer. The application running more threads than the number of cores or processors installed in the computer may slow down the application due to the effect of the thread switching overhead.

Implementing a multithreaded TCP client application

In order to turn our single-treaded client application into a multithreaded one, we need to make several changes in it. Firstly, we need to replace the `m_thread` member of the `AnyncTCPClient` class that represents a single I/O thread, with a list of pointers to the `std::thread` objects, which will represent a collection of I/O threads:

```
std::list<std::unique_ptr<std::thread>> m_threads;
```

Next, we need to change the class's constructor so that it accepts an argument representing the number of I/O threads to be created. Besides, the constructor should spawn the specified number of I/O threads and add them all to the pool of threads running the event loop:

```
AsyncTCPClient(unsigned char num_of_threads){
  m_work.reset(new boost::asio::io_service::work(m_ios));

  for (unsigned char i = 1; i <= num_of_threads; i++) {
        std::unique_ptr<std::thread> th(
            new std::thread([this](){
        m_ios.run();
      }));

    m_threads.push_back(std::move(th));
  }
}
```

Like in a single-threaded version of the client, each thread calls the `run()` method of the `m_ios` object. As a result, all threads are added to the thread pool, controlled by the `m_ios` object. All threads from the pool will be used to call the corresponding asynchronous operation completion callbacks. This means that on a multicore or multiprocessor computer, several callbacks may be running truly simultaneously in different threads, each on a separate processor; whereas, in a single-threaded version of the client, they would be executed serially.

After each thread is created, the pointer to it is put to the `m_threads` list so that we have the access to the thread objects later.

Also, the last change is in the `close()` method. Here, we need to join each thread in the list. This is how the method looks after the change:

```
void close() {
  // Destroy work object. This allows the I/O threads to
  // exit the event loop when there are no more pending
  // asynchronous operations.
  m_work.reset(NULL);

  // Waiting for the I/O threads to exit.
  for (auto& thread : m_threads) {
    thread->join();
  }
}
```

Having destroyed the `work` object, we iterate through the list of I/O threads and join each of them to make sure they all have exited.

The multithreaded TCP client application is ready. Now, when we create an object of multithreaded `AsyncTCPClient` class, the number specifying how many threads should be used to process the requests should be passed to the constructor of the class. All other aspects of usage of the class are identical to those of a single-threaded one.

See also

> ▸ *Chapter 2, I/O Operations*, includes recipes that provide detailed discussions on how to perform asynchronous I/O with TCP socket and how to cancel asynchronous operations.

> ▸ The *Using timers* recipe from *Chapter 6, Other Topics*, demonstrates how to use timers provided by Boost.Asio. Timers can be used to implement an asynchronous operation timeout mechanism.

4

Implementing Server Applications

In this chapter, we will cover the following topics:

- ▶ Implementing a synchronous iterative TCP server
- ▶ Implementing a synchronous parallel TCP server
- ▶ Implementing an asynchronous TCP server

Introduction

A **server** is a part of a distributed application that provides a service or services that are consumed by other parts of this application—**clients**. Clients communicate with the server in order to consume services provided by it.

Usually, a server application plays a passive role in the client-server communication process. During start-up, a server application attaches to a particular well-known port (meaning, it is known to the potential clients or at least it can be obtained by the clients at runtime from some well-known registry) on the host machine. After this, it passively waits for incoming requests arriving to that port from the clients. When the request arrives, the server processes it (serves) by performing actions according to the specification of the service it provides.

Depending on the services that particular server provides, the request processing may mean a different thing. An HTTP server, for example, would usually read the content of a file specified in the request message and send it back to the client. A proxy server would simply redirect a client's request to a different server for the actual processing (or maybe for another round of redirection). Other more specific servers may provide services that perform complex computations on the data provided by the client in the request and return results of such computations back to the client.

Not all servers play a passive role. Some server applications may send messages to the clients without waiting for the clients to first send a request. Usually, such servers act as *notifiers*, and they *notify* clients of some interesting events. In this case, clients may not need to send any data to the server at all. Instead, they passively wait for notifications from the server and having received one, they react accordingly. Such a communication model is called *push-style communication*. This model is gaining popularity in modern web applications, providing additional flexibility.

So, the first way to classify a server application is by the function (or functions) they perform or a service (or services) they provide to their clients.

Another obvious classification dimension is the transport layer protocol used by the server to communicate with the clients.

TCP protocol is very popular today and many general purpose server applications use it for communication. Other, more specific servers may use UDP protocol. Hybrid server applications that provide their services through both TCP and UDP protocols at the same time fall under the third category and are called **multiprotocol servers**. In this chapter, we will consider several types of TCP servers.

One more characteristic of a server is a manner in which it serves clients. An **iterative server** serves clients in one-by-one fashion, meaning that it does not start serving the next client before it completes serving the one it is currently serving. A **parallel server** can serve multiple clients in parallel. On a single-processor computer, a parallel server interleaves different stages of communication with several clients running them on a single processor. For example, having connected to one client and while waiting for the request message from it, the server can switch to connecting the second client, or read the request from the third one; after this, it can switch back to the first client to continue serving it. Such parallelism is called pseudo parallelism, as a processor is merely switching between several clients, but does not serve them truly simultaneously, which is impossible with a single processor.

On multiprocessor computers, the true parallelism is possible, when a server serves more than one client at the same time using different hardware threads for each client.

Iterative servers are relatively simple to implement and can be used when the request rate is low enough so that the server has time to finish processing one request before the next one arrives. It is clear that iterative servers are not scalable; adding more processors to the computer running such a server will not increase the server's throughput. Parallel servers, on the other hand, can handle higher request rates; if properly implemented, they are scalable. A truly parallel server running on a multiprocessor computer can handle higher request rates than the same server running on a single processor computer.

Another way to classify server applications, from an implementation's point of view, is according to whether the server is synchronous or asynchronous. A **synchronous server** uses synchronous socket API calls that block the thread of execution until the requested operation is completed, or else an error occurs. Thus, a typical synchronous TCP server would use methods such as `asio::ip::tcp::acceptor::accept()` to accept the client connection request, `asio::ip::tcp::socket::read_some()` to receive the request message from the client, and then `asio::ip::tcp::socket::write_some()` to send the response message back to the client. All three methods are blocking. They block the thread of execution until the requested operation is completed, or an error occurs, which makes the server using these operations **synchronous**.

An **asynchronous server application**, as opposed to the synchronous one, uses asynchronous socket API calls. For example, an asynchronous TCP server may use the `asio::ip::tcp::acceptor::async_accept()` method to asynchronously accept the client connection request, the `asio::ip::tcp::socket::async_read_some()` method or the `asio::async_read()` free function to asynchronously receive the request message from the client, and then the `asio::ip::tcp::socket::async_write_some()` method or the `asio::async_write()` free function to asynchronously send a response message back to the client.

Because the structure of a synchronous server application significantly differs from that of an asynchronous one, the decision as to which approach to apply should be made early at the server application design stage, and this decision should be based on the careful analysis of the application requirements. Besides, the possible application evolution paths and new requirements that may appear in the future should be considered and taken into account.

As usually, each approach has its advantages and disadvantages. When a synchronous approach yields better results in one situation, it may be absolutely unacceptable in another; in this case, an asynchronous approach might be the right choice. Let's compare two approaches to better understand the strengths and weaknesses of each of them.

The main advantage of a synchronous approach as compared to an asynchronous one is its *simplicity*. A synchronous server is significantly easier to implement, debug, and support than a functionally equal asynchronous one. Asynchronous servers are more complex due to the fact that asynchronous operations used by them complete in other places in code than they are initiated. Usually, this requires allocating additional data structures in the free memory to keep the context of the request, implementing callback functions, thread synchronization, and other extras that may make the application structure quite complex and error-prone. Most of these extras are not required in synchronous servers. Besides, an asynchronous approach brings in additional computational and memory overheads, which may make it less efficient than a synchronous one in some situations.

However, a synchronous approach has some functional limitations, which often makes it unacceptable. These limitations consist of the inability to cancel a synchronous operation after it has started, or to assign it a timeout so that it gets interrupted if it is running for too long. As opposed to synchronous operations, asynchronous ones can be canceled at any moment after the operation has been initiated.

The fact that synchronous operations cannot be canceled significantly limits the area of the application of synchronous servers. Publicly available servers that use synchronous operations are vulnerable to the attacks of a culprit. If such a server is single-threaded, a single malicious client is enough to block the server, not allowing other clients to communicate with it. Malicious client used by a culprit connects to the server and does not send any data to it, while the latter is blocked in one of the synchronous reading functions or methods, which does not allow it to serve other clients.

Such servers would usually be used in safe and protected environments in private networks, or as an internal part of an application running on a single computer using such a server for interprocess communication. Another possible application area of synchronous servers is, of course, the implementation of throwaway prototypes.

Besides the difference in the structural complexity and functionality described above, the two approaches differ in the efficiency and scalability when it comes to serving large numbers of clients sending requests at high rates. Servers using asynchronous operations are more efficient and scalable than synchronous servers especially when they run on multiprocessor computers with operating systems natively supporting an asynchronous network I/O.

The sample protocol

In this chapter, we are going to consider three recipes describing how to implement the synchronous iterative TCP server, synchronous parallel TCP server, and asynchronous TCP server. In all the recipes, it is assumed that the server communicates with clients using the following intentionally trivialized (for the sake of clarity) application layer protocol.

A server application accepts request messages represented as ASCII strings containing a sequence of symbols ending with a new-line ASCII symbol. All the symbols coming after the new-line symbol are ignored by the server.

Having received a request, the server performs some dummy operations and replies with a constant message as follows:

```
"Response\n"
```

Such a trivial protocol allows us to concentrate on the implementation of the *server* and not the *service* provided by it.

Implementing a synchronous iterative TCP server

A synchronous iterative TCP server is a part of a distributed application that satisfies the following criteria:

► Acts as a server in the client-server communication model
► Communicates with client applications over TCP protocol
► Uses I/O and control operations that block the thread of execution until the corresponding operation completes, or an error occurs
► Handles clients in a serial, one-by-one fashion

A typical synchronous iterative TCP server works according to the following algorithm:

1. Allocate an acceptor socket and bind it to a particular TCP port.
2. Run a loop until the server is stopped:
    1. Wait for the connection request from a client.
    2. Accept the client's connection request when one arrives.
    3. Wait for the request message from the client.
    4. Read the request message.
    5. Process the request.
    6. Send the response message to the client.
    7. Close the connection with the client and deallocate the socket.

This recipe demonstrates how to implement a synchronous iterative TCP server application with Boost.Asio.

How to do it...

We begin implementing our server application by defining a class responsible for handling a single client by reading the request message, processing it, and then sending back the response message. This class represents a single service provided by the server application and, therefore, we will give it a name `Service`:

```
#include <boost/asio.hpp>

#include <thread>
#include <atomic>
#include <memory>
#include <iostream>

using namespace boost;

class Service {
public:
  Service(){}

  void HandleClient(asio::ip::tcp::socket& sock) {
    try {
      asio::streambuf request;
      asio::read_until(sock, request, '\n');

      // Emulate request processing.
      inti = 0;
      while (i != 1000000)
        i++;
        std::this_thread::sleep_for(
std::chrono::milliseconds(500));

      // Sending response.
      std::string response = "Response\n";
      asio::write(sock, asio::buffer(response));
}
    catch (system::system_error&e) {
      std::cout  << "Error occured! Error code = "
<<e.code() << ". Message: "
          <<e.what();
    }
  }
};
```

To keep things simple, in our sample server application, we implement a dummy service, which only emulates the execution of certain operations. The request processing emulation consists of performing many increment operations to emulate operations that intensively consume CPU and then putting the thread of control to sleep for some time to emulate such operations as reading a file or communicating with a peripheral device synchronously.

 The Service class is quite simple and contains only one method. However, classes representing services in real-world applications would usually be more complex and richer in functionality, though the main idea would stay the same.

Next, we define another class that represents a high-level *acceptor* concept (as compared to the low-level concept represented by the asio::ip::tcp::acceptor class). This class is responsible for accepting connection requests arriving from clients and instantiating objects of the Service class, which will provide the service to the connected clients. Let's name this class correspondingly—Acceptor:

```
class Acceptor {
public:
  Acceptor(asio::io_service&ios, unsigned short port_num) :
    m_ios(ios),
    m_acceptor(m_ios,
        asio::ip::tcp::endpoint(
            asio::ip::address_v4::any(),
            port_num))
  {
    m_acceptor.listen();
  }

  void Accept() {
    asio::ip::tcp::socket sock(m_ios);

    m_acceptor.accept(sock);

    Service svc;
    svc.HandleClient(sock);
  }

private:
  asio::io_service&m_ios;
  asio::ip::tcp::acceptor m_acceptor;
};
```

This class owns an object of the `asio::ip::tcp::acceptor` class named `m_acceptor`, which is used to synchronously accept incoming connection requests.

Also, we define a class that represents the server itself. The class is named correspondingly—`Server`:

```
class Server {
public:
  Server() : m_stop(false) {}

  void Start(unsigned short port_num) {
    m_thread.reset(new std::thread([this, port_num]() {
      Run(port_num);
    }));
  }

  void Stop() {
    m_stop.store(true);
    m_thread->join();
  }

private:
  void Run(unsigned short port_num) {
    Acceptor acc(m_ios, port_num);

    while (!m_stop.load()) {
      acc.Accept();
    }
  }

  std::unique_ptr<std::thread>m_thread;
  std::atomic<bool>m_stop;
  asio::io_servicem_ios;
};
```

This class provides an interface comprised by two methods—`Start()` and `Stop()` that are used to start and stop the server correspondingly. The loop runs in a separate tread spawned by the `Start()` method. The `Start()` method is nonblocking, while the `Stop()` method blocks the caller thread until the server is stopped.

Thorough inspection of the `Server` class reveals one serious drawback of the implementation of the server—the `Stop()` method may never return under some circumstances. The discussion of this problem and the ways to resolve it is provided later in this recipe.

Eventually, we implement the application entry point function `main()` that demonstrates how to use the `Server` class:

```
int main()
{
  unsigned short port_num = 3333;

  try {
    Server srv;
    srv.Start(port_num);

    std::this_thread::sleep_for(std::chrono::seconds(60));

    srv.Stop();
  }
  catch (system::system_error&e) {
        std::cout   << "Error occured! Error code = "
                    <<e.code() << ". Message: "
                    <<e.what();
  }

  return 0;
}
```

How it works...

The sample server application consists of four components—the `Server`, `Acceptor`, and `Service` classes and the application entry point function `main()`. Let's consider how each of these components work.

The Service class

The `Service` class is the key functional component in the whole application. While other components are infrastructural in their purpose, this class implements the actual function (or service) provided by the server to the clients.

This class is simple and consists of a single `HandleClient()` method. This method accepts an object representing a socket connected to the client as its input argument and handles that particular client.

In our sample, such handling is trivial. Firstly, the request message is synchronously read from the socket until a new line ASCII symbol \n is encountered. Then, the request is processed. In our case, we emulate processing by running a dummy loop performing one million increment operations and then putting the thread to sleep for half a second. After this, the response message is prepared and synchronously sent back to the client.

The exceptions that may be thrown by Boost.Asio I/O functions and methods are caught and handled in the `HandleClient()` method and are not propagated to the method caller so that if the handling of one client fails, the server continues working.

Depending on the needs of a particular application, the `Service` class can be extended and enriched with a functionality to provide the needed service.

The Acceptor class

The `Acceptor` class is a part of the server application infrastructure. When constructed, it instantiates an acceptor socket object `m_acceptor` and calls its `listen()` method to start listening for connection requests from clients.

This class exposes a single public method named `Accept()`. This method when called, instantiates an object of the `asio::ip::tcp::socket` class named `sock`, representing an active socket, and tries to accept a connection request. If there are pending connection requests available, the connection request is processed and the active socket `sock` is connected to the new client. Otherwise, this method blocks until a new connection request arrives.

Then, an instance of the `Service` object is created and its `HandleClient()` method is called. The `sock` object connected to the client is passed to this method. The `HandleClient()` method blocks until communication with the client and request processing completes, or an error occurs. When the `HandleClient()` method returns, the `Accept()` method of the `Acceptor` class returns too. Now, *the acceptor* is ready to accept the next connection request.

One execution of the class's `Accept()` method performs the full handling cycle of one client.

The Server class

The `Server` class, as its name suggests, represents a *server* that can be controlled through class's interface methods `Start()` and `Stop()`.

The `Start()` method initiates the start-up of the server. It spawns a new thread, which starts its execution from the `Server` class's `Run()` private method and returns. The `Run()` method accepts a single argument named `port_num` specifying the number of protocol port on which the acceptor socket should listen for incoming connection requests. When invoked, the method first instantiates an object of the `Acceptor` class and then starts a loop in which the `Accept()` method of the `Acceptor` object is called. The loop terminates when the value of the `m_stop` atomic variable becomes `true`, which happens when the `Stop()` method is invoked on the corresponding instance of the `Server` class.

The Stop() method synchronously stops the server. It does not return until the loop started in the Run() method is interrupted and the thread spawned by the Start() method finishes its execution. To interrupt the loop, the value of the atomic variable m_stop is set to true. After this, the Stop() method calls the join() method on the m_thread object representing the thread running the loop in the Run() method to wait until it exits the loop and finishes its execution.

The presented implementation has a significant drawback consisting in the fact that the server may not be stopped immediately. More than that, there is a possibility that the server will not be stopped at all and the Stop() method will block its caller forever. The root cause of the problem is that the server has a hard dependency on the behavior of the clients.

If the Stop() method is called and the value of the atomic variable m_stop is set to true just before the loop termination condition in the Run() method is checked, the server is stopped almost immediately and no problem appears. However, if the Stop() method is called while the server's thread is blocked in the acc.Accept() method waiting for the next connection request from the client, or in one of the synchronous I/O operations inside the Service class waiting for the request message from the connected client, or for the client to receive the response message, the server cannot be stopped until these blocking operations are completed. Hence, for example, if at the moment, when the Stop() method is called, there are no pending connection requests, the server will not be stopped until a new client connects and gets handled, which in general case may never happen and will lead to the server being blocked forever.

Later, in this section, we will consider the possible ways to tackle this drawback.

The main() entry point function

This function demonstrates the usage of the server. It creates an instance of the Server class named srv and calls its Start() method to start the server. Because the server is represented as an active object running in its own thread of control, the Start() method returns immediately and the thread running method main() continues execution. To let the server run for some time, the main thread is put to sleep for 60 seconds. After the main thread wakes up, it calls the Stop() method on the srv object to stop the server. When the Stop() method returns, the main() function returns too and our sample application exits.

Of course, in the real application, the server would be stopped as a reaction to a user input or any other relevant event, rather than after dummy 60 seconds, after the server's start-up run out.

Eliminating the drawbacks

As it has already been mentioned, the presented implementation has two drawbacks that significantly limit its applicability. The first problem is that it may be impossible to stop the server if the `Stop()` method is called while the server thread is blocked waiting for the incoming connection request, no connection requests arrive. The second problem is that the server can be easily hung by a single malicious (or buggy) client, making it unavailable to other clients. To hang the server, the client application can simply connect to the server and never send any request to it, which will make the server application hang in the blocking input operation forever.

The root cause of both the issues is the usage of blocking operations in the server (which is natural for synchronous servers). A reasonable and simple solution to both these issues would be to assign a timeout to the blocking operations, which would guarantee that the server would unblock periodically to check whether the stop command has been issued and also to forcefully discard clients that do not send requests for a long period of time. However, Boost.Asio does not provide a way to cancel synchronous operations, or to assign timeouts to them. Therefore, we should try to find other ways to make our synchronous server more responsive and stable.

Let's consider ways to tackle each of the two drawbacks.

Stopping a server in reasonable amount of time

As the only legitimate way to make the `accept()` synchronous method of an acceptor socket unblock when there are no pending connection requests is to send a dummy connection request to the port on which the acceptor is listening, we can do the following trick to solve our problem.

In the `Server` class's `Stop()` method, after setting the value of the `m_stop` atomic variable to `true`, we can create a dummy active socket, connect it to this same server, and send some dummy request. This will guarantee that the server thread will leave the `accept()` method of the acceptor socket and will eventually check the value of the `m_stop` atomic variable to find out that its value is equal to `true`, which will lead to termination of the loop and completion of the `Acceptor::Accept()` method.

In the described method, it is assumed that the server stops itself by sending a message to itself (actually a message is sent from an I/O thread to the worker thread). Another approach would be to have a special client (separate application) that would connect and send a special service message (for example, `stop\n`) to the server, which will be interpreted by the server as a signal to stop. In this case, the server would be controlled externally (from a different application) and the `Server` class would not need to have the `Stop()` method.

Dealing with the server's vulnerability

Unfortunately, the nature of blocking the I/O operation without the timeout assigned to it is such that it can be used to easily hang the iterative server that uses such operations and make it inaccessible to other clients.

Obviously, to protect the server from this vulnerability, we need to redesign it so that it never gets blocked by I/O operations. One way to achieve this is to use nonblocking sockets (which will turn our server into reactive) or use asynchronous I/O operations. Both the options mean that our server stops being synchronous. We will consider some of these solutions in other recipes of this chapter.

Analyzing the results

Vulnerabilities that are inherent in the synchronous iterative servers implemented with Boost.Asio described above do not allow using them in public networks, where there is a risk of misuse of the server by a culprit. Usually, synchronous servers would be used in closed and protected environments where clients are carefully designed so that they do not hang the server.

Another limitation of the iterative synchronous server is that they are not scalable and cannot take advantage of a multiprocessor hardware. However, their advantage—simplicity—is the reason why this type of a server is a good choice in many cases.

See also

- ▶ *Chapter 2, I/O Operations*, includes recipes providing detailed discussions on how to perform synchronous I/O.

Implementing a synchronous parallel TCP server

A synchronous parallel TCP server is a part of a distributed application that satisfies the following criteria:

- ▶ Acts as a server in the client-server communication model
- ▶ Communicates with client applications over TCP protocol
- ▶ Uses I/O and control operations that block the thread of execution until the corresponding operation completes, or an error occurs
- ▶ May handle more than one client simultaneously

A typical synchronous parallel TCP server works according to the following algorithm:

1. Allocate an acceptor socket and bind it to a particular TCP port.
2. Run a loop until the server is stopped:

   ❑ Wait for the incoming connection request from a client

   ❑ Accept the client's connection request

   ❑ Spawn a thread of control and in the context of this thread:

      ❑ Wait for the request message from the client

      ❑ Read the request message

      ❑ Process the request

      ❑ Send a response message to the client

      ❑ Close the connection with the client and deallocate the socket

This recipe demonstrates how to implement a synchronous parallel TCP server application with Boost.Asio.

How to do it...

We begin implementing our server application by defining the class responsible for handling a single client by reading the request message, processing it, and then sending back the response message. This class represents a single service provided by the server application and, therefore, we will name it `Service`:

```cpp
#include <boost/asio.hpp>

#include <thread>
#include <atomic>
#include <memory>
#include <iostream>

using namespace boost;

class Service {
public:
   Service(){}

   void StartHandligClient(
         std::shared_ptr<asio::ip::tcp::socket> sock) {
```

```
            std::thread th((([this, sock]() {
                HandleClient(sock);
            })));

            th.detach();
        }

    private:
    void HandleClient(std::shared_ptr<asio::ip::tcp::socket> sock) {
            try {
                asio::streambuf request;
                asio::read_until(*sock.get(), request, '\n');

                // Emulate request processing.
                int i = 0;
                while (i != 1000000)
                    i++;

                    std::this_thread::sleep_for(
std::chrono::milliseconds(500));

                // Sending response.
                std::string response = "Response\n";
                asio::write(*sock.get(), asio::buffer(response));
            }
            catch (system::system_error &e) {
                std::cout    << "Error occured! Error code = "
<< e.code() << ". Message: "
                        << e.what();
            }

            // Clean-up.
            delete this;
        }
    };
```

To keep things simple, in our sample server application, we implement a dummy service, which only emulates the execution of certain operations. The request processing emulation consists of performing many increment operations to emulate operations that intensively consume CPU and then putting the thread of control to sleep for some time to emulate I/O operations such as reading a file or communicating with a peripheral device synchronously.

The `Service` class is quite simple and contains only one method. However, classes representing services in real-world applications would usually be more complex and richer in functionality, though the main idea would stay the same.

Next, we define another class that represents a high-level *acceptor* concept (as compared to the low-level concept represented by the `asio::ip::tcp::acceptor` class). This class is responsible for accepting the connection requests arriving from clients and instantiating the objects of the `Service` class, which will provide the service to connected clients. Let's name it Acceptor:

```cpp
class Acceptor {
public:
    Acceptor(asio::io_service& ios, unsigned short port_num) :
        m_ios(ios),
        m_acceptor(m_ios,
            asio::ip::tcp::endpoint(
asio::ip::address_v4::any(),
port_num))
    {
        m_acceptor.listen();
    }

    void Accept() {
        std::shared_ptr<asio::ip::tcp::socket>
sock(new asio::ip::tcp::socket(m_ios));

        m_acceptor.accept(*sock.get());

        (new Service)->StartHandligClient(sock);
    }

private:
    asio::io_service& m_ios;
    asio::ip::tcp::acceptor m_acceptor;
};
```

This class owns an object of the `asio::ip::tcp::acceptor` class named `m_acceptor`, which is used to synchronously accept incoming connection requests.

Also, we define a class that represents the server itself. The class is named correspondingly—`Server`:

```
class Server {
public:
  Server() : m_stop(false) {}

  void Start(unsigned short port_num) {
    m_thread.reset(new std::thread([this, port_num]() {
      Run(port_num);
    }));
  }

  void Stop() {
    m_stop.store(true);
    m_thread->join();
  }

private:
  void Run(unsigned short port_num) {
    Acceptor acc(m_ios, port_num);

    while (!m_stop.load()) {
      acc.Accept();
    }
  }

  std::unique_ptr<std::thread>m_thread;
  std::atomic<bool>m_stop;
  asio::io_servicem_ios;
};
```

This class provides an interface comprised of two methods—`Start()` and `Stop()` that are used to start and stop the server correspondingly. The loop runs in a separate thread spawned by the `Start()` method. The `Start()` method is nonblocking, while the `Stop()` method is. It blocks the caller thread until the server is stopped.

Thorough inspection of the `Server` class reveals one serious drawback of the implementation of the server—the `Stop()` method may block forever. The discussion of this problem and ways to resolve it is provided below.

Eventually, we implement the application entry point function `main()` that demonstrates how to use the `Server` class:

```
int main()
{
    unsigned short port_num = 3333;

    try {
        Server srv;
        srv.Start(port_num);

        std::this_thread::sleep_for(std::chrono::seconds(60));

        srv.Stop();
    }
    catch (system::system_error &e) {
        std::cout    << "Error occured! Error code = "
<< e.code() << ". Message: "
            << e.what();
    }

    return 0;
}
```

How it works...

The sample server application consists of four components—the `Server`, `Acceptor`, and `Service` classes and the application entry point function `main()`. Let's consider how each of these components work.

The Service class

The `Service` class is the key functional component in the whole application. While other components constitute the infrastructure of the server, this class implements the actual function (or service) provided by the server to the clients.

This class has a single method in its interface called `StartHandlingClient()`. This method accepts a pointer to an object representing a TCP socket connected to the client as its input argument and starts handling that particular client.

This method spawns a thread of control, which starts its execution from the class's `HandleClient()` private method, where the actual synchronous handling is performed. Having spawned the thread, the `StartHandlingClient()` method "lets it go" by detaching the thread from the `std::thread` object representing it. After this, the `StartHandlingClient()` method returns.

The `HandleClient()` private method, as its name suggests, handles the client. In our sample, such handling is trivial. Firstly, the request message is synchronously read from the socket until a new line ASCII symbol \n is encountered. Then, the request is processed. In our case, we emulate processing by running a dummy loop performing one million increment operations and then putting the thread to sleep for half a second. After this, the response message is prepared and sent back to the client.

When the response message is sent, the object of the `Service` class associated with the `HandleClient()` method, which is currently running, is deleted by the `delete` operator. Of course, the design of the class assumes that its instances will be allocated in free memory by a `new` operator rather than on the stack.

Depending on the needs of a particular application, the `Service` class can be extended and enriched with the functionality to provide the needed service.

The Acceptor class

The `Acceptor` class is a part of the server application infrastructure. When constructed, it instantiates an acceptor socket object `m_acceptor` and calls its `listen()` method to start listening for connection requests from clients.

This class exposes a single `Accept()` public method. This method when called, instantiates an object of the `asio::ip::tcp::socket` class named `sock`, representing an active socket, and tries to accept a connection request. If there are pending connection requests available, the connection request is processed and the active socket `sock` is connected to the new client. Otherwise, this method blocks until a new connection request arrives.

Then, an instance of the `Service` object is allocated in free memory and its `StartHandlingClient()` method is called. The `sock` object is passed to this method as an input argument. The `StartHandlingClient()` method spawns a thread in the context of which the client will be handled and returns immediately. When the `StartHandlingClient()` method returns, the `Accept()` method of the `Acceptor` class returns too. Now, *the acceptor* is ready to accept the next connection request.

Note that `Acceptor` does not take the ownership of the object of the `Service` class. Instead, the object of the `Service` class will destroy itself when it completes its job.

The Server class

The `Server` class, as its name suggests, represents a *server* that can be controlled through the class's interface `Start()` and `Stop()` methods.

The `Start()` method initiates the start-up of the server. It spawns a new thread that begins its execution from the `Server` class's `Run()` private method and returns. The `Run()` method accepts a single argument `port_num` specifying the number of the protocol port on which the acceptor socket should listen for incoming connection requests. When invoked, the method first instantiates an object of the `Acceptor` class and then starts a loop in which the `Accept()` method of the `Acceptor` object is called. The loop terminates when the value of the `m_stop` atomic variable becomes `true`, which happens when the `Stop()` method is invoked on the corresponding instance of the `Server` class.

The `Stop()` method synchronously stops the server. It does not return until a loop that started in the `Run()` method is interrupted and the thread that is spawned by the `Start()` method finishes its execution. To interrupt the loop, the value of the atomic variable `m_stop` is set to `true`. After this, the `Stop()` method calls the `join()` method on the `m_thread` object representing the thread running the loop in the `Run()` method in order to wait until it finishes its execution.

The presented implementation has a significant drawback consisting of the fact that the server may not be stopped immediately. More than that, there is a possibility that the server will not be stopped at all and the `Stop()` method will block its caller forever. The root cause of the problem is that the server has a hard dependency on the behavior of the clients.

If the `Stop()` method is called and sets the value of atomic variable `m_stop` variable to `true` just before the loop termination condition in the `Run()` method is checked, the server is stopped almost immediately and no problem occurs. However, if the `Stop()` method is called while the server's thread is blocked in the `acc.Accept()` method waiting for the next connection request from the client—or in one of synchronous I/O operations inside the `Service` class is waiting for the request message from the connected client or for the client to receive the response message—the server cannot be stopped until these blocking operations complete. Hence, for example, if at the moment when the `Stop()` method is called, there are no pending connection requests, the server will not be stopped until a new client connects and gets handled, which in general case may never happen and may lead to the server being blocked forever.

Later, in this section, we will consider possible ways to tackle this drawback.

The main() entry point function

This function demonstrates the usage of the server. It creates an instance of the `Server` class named `srv` and calls its method `Start()` to start the server. Because the server is represented as an active object running in its own thread of control, the `Start()` method returns immediately and the thread running the `main()` method continues the execution. To allow the server to run for some time, the main thread is put to sleep for 60 seconds. After the main thread wakes up, it calls the `Stop()` method on the `srv` object to stop the server. When the `Stop()` method returns, the `main()` function returns too and our sample application exits.

Of course, in the real application, the server would be stopped as a reaction to the user input or any other relevant event, rather than after the dummy 60 seconds after the server's start-up run out.

Eliminating the drawbacks

The drawbacks inherent in synchronous parallel server application implemented with Boost. Asio library are similar to those of synchronous iterative server application considered in previous recipe. Please refer to the *Implementing synchronous iterative TCP server* recipe for the discussion of the drawbacks and the ways to eliminate them.

See also

 ▸ Recipe *Implementing synchronous iterative TCP server* provides more details on the drawbacks inherent in both synchronous iterative and synchronous parallel servers and the possible ways to eliminate them

 ▸ *Chapter 2, I/O Operations*, includes recipes providing detailed discussions on how to perform synchronous I/O

Implementing an asynchronous TCP server

An asynchronous TCP server is a part of a distributed application that satisfies the following criteria:

 ▸ Acts as a server in the client-server communication model

 ▸ Communicates with client applications over TCP protocol

 ▸ Uses the asynchronous I/O and control operations

 ▸ May handle multiple clients simultaneously

A typical asynchronous TCP server works according to the following algorithm:

1. Allocate an acceptor socket and bind it to a particular TCP port.

2. Initiate the asynchronous accept operation.

3. Spawn one or more threads of control and add them to the pool of threads that run the Boost.Asio event loop.

4. When the asynchronous accept operation completes, initiate a new one to accept the next connection request.

5. Initiate the asynchronous reading operation to read the request from the connected client.

6. When the asynchronous reading operation completes, process the request and prepare the response message.

7. Initiate the asynchronous writing operation to send the response message to the client.

8. When the asynchronous writing operation completes, close the connection and deallocate the socket.

Note that the steps starting from the fourth step in the preceding algorithm may be performed in arbitrary order depending on the relative timing of the concrete asynchronous operations in a concrete application. Due to the asynchronous model of the server, sequential order of execution of the steps may not hold even when the server is running on a single-processor computer.

This recipe demonstrates how to implement an asynchronous TCP server application with Boost.Asio.

How to do it...

We begin implementing our server application by defining a class responsible for handling a single client by reading the request message, processing it, and then sending back the response message. This class represents a single service provided by the server application. Let's name it `Service`:

```
#include <boost/asio.hpp>

#include <thread>
#include <atomic>
#include <memory>
#include <iostream>

using namespace boost;
```

```
class Service {
public:
    Service(std::shared_ptr<asio::ip::tcp::socket> sock) :
        m_sock(sock)
    {}

    void StartHandling() {

        asio::async_read_until(*m_sock.get(),
            m_request,
            '\n',
            [this](
                        const boost::system::error_code& ec,
                        std::size_t bytes_transferred)
                        {
                                onRequestReceived(ec,
                                 bytes_transferred);
                }); 
    }

private:
    void onRequestReceived(const boost::system::error_code& ec,
                std::size_t bytes_transferred) {
        if (ec != 0) {
            std::cout << "Error occured! Error code = "
                << ec.value()
                << ". Message: " << ec.message();

            onFinish();
                return;
        }

// Process the request.
        m_response = ProcessRequest(m_request);

        // Initiate asynchronous write operation.
        asio::async_write(*m_sock.get(),
            asio::buffer(m_response),
            [this](
                        const boost::system::error_code& ec,
                        std::size_t bytes_transferred)
                        {
                    onResponseSent(ec,
                            bytes_transferred);
```

```cpp
                   });
    }

    void onResponseSent(const boost::system::error_code& ec,
                        std::size_t bytes_transferred) {
        if (ec != 0) {
            std::cout << "Error occured! Error code = "
                << ec.value()
                << ". Message: " << ec.message();
        }

        onFinish();
    }

    // Here we perform the cleanup.
    void onFinish() {
        delete this;
    }

    std::string ProcessRequest(asio::streambuf& request) {

        // In this method we parse the request, process it
        // and prepare the request.

        // Emulate CPU-consuming operations.
        int i = 0;
        while (i != 1000000)
            i++;

        // Emulate operations that block the thread
// (e.g. synch I/O operations).
        std::this_thread::sleep_for(
                        std::chrono::milliseconds(100));

        // Prepare and return the response message.
        std::string response = "Response\n";
        return response;
    }

private:
    std::shared_ptr<asio::ip::tcp::socket> m_sock;
    std::string m_response;
    asio::streambuf m_request;
};
```

To keep things simple, in our sample server application, we implement a dummy service which only emulates the execution of certain operations. The request processing emulation consists of performing many increment operations to emulate operations that intensively consume CPU and then putting the thread of control to sleep for some time to emulate I/O operations such as reading a file or communicating with a peripheral device synchronously.

Each instance of the `Service` class is intended to handle one connected client by reading the request message, processing it, and then sending the response message back.

Next, we define another class, which represents a high-level *acceptor* concept (as compared to the low-level concept represented by the `asio::ip::tcp::acceptor` class). This class is responsible for accepting the connection requests arriving from clients and instantiating the objects of the `Service` class, which will provide the service to connected clients. Let's name it `Acceptor`:

```cpp
class Acceptor {
public:
  Acceptor(asio::io_service&ios, unsigned short port_num)  :
    m_ios(ios),
    m_acceptor(m_ios,
      asio::ip::tcp::endpoint(
                  asio::ip::address_v4::any(),
                  port_num)),
    m_isStopped(false)
  {}

  // Start accepting incoming connection requests.
  void Start() {
    m_acceptor.listen();
    InitAccept();
  }

  // Stop accepting incoming connection requests.
  void Stop() {
    m_isStopped.store(true);
  }

private:
  void InitAccept() {
    std::shared_ptr<asio::ip::tcp::socket>
            sock(new asio::ip::tcp::socket(m_ios));

    m_acceptor.async_accept(*sock.get(),
      [this, sock](
```

```
                    const boost::system::error_code& error)
            {
          onAccept(error, sock);
        });
  }

    void onAccept(const boost::system::error_code&ec,
              std::shared_ptr<asio::ip::tcp::socket> sock)
  {
    if (ec == 0) {
      (new Service(sock))->StartHandling();
    }
    else {
      std::cout<< "Error occured! Error code = "
        <<ec.value()
        << ". Message: " <<ec.message();
    }

    // Init next async accept operation if
    // acceptor has not been stopped yet.
    if (!m_isStopped.load()) {
      InitAccept();
    }
    else {
      // Stop accepting incoming connections
      // and free allocated resources.
      m_acceptor.close();
    }
  }

private:
  asio::io_service&m_ios;
  asio::ip::tcp::acceptor m_acceptor;
  std::atomic<bool>m_isStopped;
};
```

This class owns an object of the `asio::ip::tcp::acceptor` class named `m_acceptor`, which is used to asynchronously accept the incoming connection requests.

Also, we define a class that represents the server itself. The class is named correspondingly—`Server`:

```cpp
class Server {
public:
  Server() {
    m_work.reset(new asio::io_service::work(m_ios));
  }

  // Start the server.
  void Start(unsigned short port_num,
unsigned int thread_pool_size) {

    assert(thread_pool_size > 0);

    // Create and start Acceptor.
    acc.reset(new Acceptor(m_ios, port_num));
    acc->Start();

    // Create specified number of threads and
    // add them to the pool.
    for (unsigned int i = 0; i < thread_pool_size; i++) {
      std::unique_ptr<std::thread> th(
              new std::thread([this]()
              {
                    m_ios.run();
              }));

      m_thread_pool.push_back(std::move(th));
    }
  }

  // Stop the server.
  void Stop() {
    acc->Stop();
    m_ios.stop();

    for (auto& th : m_thread_pool) {
      th->join();
    }
  }
```

```
    private:
      asio::io_servicem_ios;
      std::unique_ptr<asio::io_service::work>m_work;
      std::unique_ptr<Acceptor>acc;
      std::vector<std::unique_ptr<std::thread>>m_thread_pool;
  };
```

This class provides an interface consisting of two methods—Start() and Stop(). The Start() method accepts a protocol port number on which the server should listen for the incoming connection requests and the number of threads to add to the pool as input arguments and starts the server. The Stop() method stops the server. The Start() method is nonblocking, while the Stop() method is. It blocks the caller thread until the server is stopped and all the threads running the event loop exit.

Eventually, we implement the application entry point function main() that demonstrates how to use an object of the Server class:

```
const unsigned intDEFAULT_THREAD_POOL_SIZE = 2;

int main()
{
  unsigned short port_num = 3333;

  try {
    Server srv;

    unsigned intthread_pool_size =
      std::thread::hardware_concurrency() * 2;

      if (thread_pool_size == 0)
      thread_pool_size = DEFAULT_THREAD_POOL_SIZE;

    srv.Start(port_num, thread_pool_size);

    std::this_thread::sleep_for(std::chrono::seconds(60));

    srv.Stop();
  }
  catch (system::system_error&e) {
    std::cout  << "Error occured! Error code = "
               <<e.code() << ". Message: "
               <<e.what();
  }

  return 0;
}
```

How it works...

The sample server application consists of four components—the `Service`, `Acceptor`, and `Service` classes and an application entry point function `main()`. Let's consider how each of these components work.

The Service class

The `Service` class is the key functional component in the application. While other components constitute an infrastructure of the server, this class implements the actual function (or service) provided by the server to the clients.

One instance of this class is intended to handle a single connected client by reading the request, processing it, and then sending back the response message.

The class's constructor accepts a shared pointer to an object representing a socket connected to a particular client as an argument and caches this pointer. This socket will be used later to communicate with the client application.

The public interface of the `Service` class consists of a single method `StartHandling()`. This method starts handling the client by initiating the asynchronous reading operation to read the request message from the client specifying the `onRequestReceived()` method as a callback. Having initiated the asynchronous reading operation, the `StartHandling()` method returns.

When the request reading completes, or an error occurs, the callback method `onRequestReceived()` is called. This method first checks whether the reading succeeded by testing the `ec` argument that contains the operation completion status code. In case the reading finished with an error, the corresponding message is output to the standard output stream and then the `onFinish()` method is called. After this, the `onRequestReceieved()` method returns, which leads to client-handling process interruption.

If the request message has been read successfully, the `ProcessRequest()` method is called to perform the requested operations and prepare the response message. When the `ProcessRequest()` method completes and returns the string containing the response message, the asynchronous writing operation is initiated to send this response message back to the client. The `onResponseSent()` method is specified as a callback.

When the writing operation completes (or an error occurs), the `onResponseSent()` method is called. This method first checks whether the operation succeeded. If the operation failed, the corresponding message is output to the standard output stream. Next, the `onFinish()` method is called to perform the cleanup. When the `onFinish()` method returns, the full cycle of client handling is considered completed.

The `ProcessRequest()` method is the heart of the class because it implements the service. In our server application, we have a dummy service that runs a dummy loop performing one million increment operations and then puts the thread to sleep for 100 milliseconds. After this, the dummy response message is generated and returned to the caller.

Depending on the needs of a particular application, the `Service` class and particularly its `ProcessRequest()` method can be extended and enriched with a functionality to provide the needed service.

The `Service` class is designed so that its objects delete themselves when their job is completed. Deletion is performed in the class's `onFinish()` private method, which is called in the end of the client handling cycle whether it is successful or erroneous:

```
void onFinish() {
  delete this;
}
```

The Acceptor class

The `Acceptor` class is a part of the server application's infrastructure. Its constructor accepts a port number on which it will listen for the incoming connection requests as its input argument. The object of this class contains an instance of the `asio::ip::tcp::acceptor` class as its member named `m_acceptor`, which is constructed in the `Acceptor` class's constructor.

The `Acceptor` class exposes two public methods—`Start()` and `Stop()`. The `Start()` method is intended to instruct an object of the `Acceptor` class to start listening and accepting incoming connection requests. It puts the `m_acceptor` acceptor socket into listening mode and then calls the class's `InitAccept()` private method. The `InitAccept()` method, in turn, constructs an active socket object and initiates the asynchronous accept operation, calling the `async_accept()` method on the acceptor socket object and passing the object representing an active socket to it as an argument. The `onAccept()` method of the `Acceptor` class is specified as a callback.

When the connection request is accepted or an error occurs, the callback method `onAccept()` is called. This method first checks whether any error occurred while the asynchronous operation was executed by checking the value of its input argument `ec`. If the operation completed successfully, an instance of the `Service` class is created and its `StartHandling()` method is called, which starts handling the connected client. Otherwise, in case of error, the corresponding message is output to the standard output stream.

Next, the value of the `m_isStopped` atomic variable is checked to see whether the stop command has been issued on the `Acceptor` object. If it has (which means that the `Stop()` method has been called on the `Acceptor` object), a new asynchronous accept operation is not initiated and the low-level acceptor object is closed. At this point, `Acceptor` stops listening and accepting incoming connection requests from clients. Otherwise, the `InitAccept()` method is called to initiate a new asynchronous accept operation to accept the next incoming connection request.

As it has already been mentioned, the `Stop()` method instructs the `Acceptor` object not to initiate the next asynchronous accept operation when the currently running one completes. However, the currently running accept operation is not canceled by this method.

The Server class

The `Server` class, as its name suggests, represents a *server* itself. The class's public interface consists of two methods: `Start()` and `Stop()`.

The `Start()` method starts the server up. It accepts two arguments. The first argument named `port_num` specifies the number of the protocol port on which the server should listen for incoming connections. The second argument named `thread_pool_size` specifies the number of threads to add to the pool of threads running the even loop and deliver asynchronous operation completion events. This argument is very important and should be chosen with care as it directly influences the performance of the server.

The `Start()` method begins by instantiating an object of the `Acceptor` class that will be used to accept incoming connections and then starting it up by calling its `Start()` method. After this, it spawns a set of worker threads, each of which is added to the pool, by calling the `run()` method of the `asio::io_service` object. Besides, all the `std::thread` objects are cached in the `m_thread_pool` member vector so that the corresponding threads can be joined later when the server is stopped.

The `Stop()` method first stops the `Acceptor` object acc, calling its `Stop()` method. Then, it calls the `stop()` method on the `asio::io_service` object m_ios, which makes all the threads that previously called `m_ios.run()` to join the pool to exit as soon as possible, discarding all pending asynchronous operations. After this, the `Stop()` method waits for all threads in the pool to exit by iterating through all the `std::thread` objects cached in the `m_thread_pool` vector and joining each of them.

When all threads exit, the `Stop()` method returns.

The main() entry point function

This function demonstrates the usage of the server. Firstly, it instantiates an object of the `Server` class named srv. Because the `Start()` method of the `Server` class requires a number of threads constituting a pool to be passed to it, before starting the server, the optimal size of the pool is calculated. The general formula often used in parallel applications to find the optimal number of threads is the number of processors the computer has multiplied by 2. We use the `std::thread::hardware_concurrency()` static method to obtain the number of processors. However, because this method may fail to do its job returning 0, we fall back to default value represented by the constant DEFAULT_THREAD_POOL_SIZE, which is equal to 2 in our case.

When the thread pool size is calculated, the `Start()` method is called to start the server. The `Start()` method does not block. When it returns, the thread running the `main()` method continues the execution. To allow the server to run for some time, the main thread is put to sleep for 60 seconds. When the main thread wakes up, it calls the `Stop()` method on the `srv` object to stop the server. When the `Stop()` method returns, the `main()` function returns too and our application exits.

Of course, in the real application, the server would be stopped as a reaction to some relevant event such as the user input, rather than when some dummy period of time elapses.

See also

- ▸ *Chapter 2, I/O Operations*, includes recipes providing detailed discussions on how to perform synchronous I/O.

- ▸ The *Using timers* recipe from *Chapter 6, Other Topics*, demonstrates how to use timers provided by Boost.Asio. Timers can be used to implement an asynchronous operation timeout mechanism.

5

HTTP and SSL/TLS

In this chapter, we will cover the following topics:

- ► Implementing the HTTP client application
- ► Implementing the HTTP server application
- ► Adding SSL/TLS support to client applications
- ► Adding SSL/TLS support to server applications

Introduction

This chapter covers two major topics. The first one is HTTP protocol implementation. The second is the usage of SSL/TLS protocol. Let's briefly examine each of them.

The **HTTP protocol** is an application layer protocol operating on the top of TCP protocol. It is widely used on the Internet, allowing client applications to request particular resources from the servers, and servers to transmit the requested resources back to the clients. Besides, HTTP allows clients to upload data and send commands to the server.

The HTTP protocol assumes several models or **methods** of communication, each designed for a specific purpose. The simplest method called GET assumes the following flow of events:

1. The HTTP client application (for example, a web browser) generates a request message containing information about a particular resource (residing on the server) to be requested and sends it to the HTTP server application (for example, a web server) using TCP as a transport level protocol.

2. The HTTP server application, having received a request from the client, parses it, extracts the requested resource from the storage (for example, from a file system or a database), and sends it back to the client as a part of a HTTP response message.

The format of both the request and response messages is defined by HTTP protocol.

Several other methods are defined by HTTP protocol, allowing client application to actively send data or upload resources to the server, delete resources located on the server, and perform other operations. In the recipes of this chapter, we will consider implementation of the GET method. Because HTTP protocol methods are similar in principle, implementation of one of them gives a good hint about how to implement others.

Another topic covered in this chapter is **SSL and TLS protocols**. **Secure Socket Layer** (**SSL**) and **Transport Layer Security** (**TLS**) protocols operate on the top of TCP protocol and are aimed at achieving two main goals as follows:

- Providing a way to authenticate each communication participant using digital certificate
- Securing data being transmitted over the underlying TCP protocol

The SSL and TLS protocols are widespread, especially in the Web. Most web servers to which its potential clients may send sensitive data (passwords, credit card numbers, personal data, and so on) support SSL/TLS-enabled communication. In this case, the so called HTTPS (HTTP over SSL) protocol is used to allow the client to authenticate the server (sometimes servers may want to authenticate the client, though this is rarely the case) and to secure transmitted data by encrypting it, making this data useless for the culprit even if intercepted.

Boost.Asio does not contain the implementation of SSL/TLS protocols. Instead, it relies on the OpenSSL library. Boost.Asio provides a set of classes, functions, and data structures that facilitate the usage of functionality provided by OpenSSL, making the code of the application more uniformed and object-oriented.

In this chapter, we will not consider the details of the OpenSSL library or SSL/TLS protocols. These topics are not in the scope of this book. Instead, we will touch upon specific tools provided by the Boost.Asio that rely on OpenSSL library and allow to implement support of SSL/TLS protocol in a network application.

The two recipes demonstrate how to build client and server applications that secure their communication using SSL/TLS protocols. To make SSL/TLS-related aspects of the applications more vivid and clear, all other aspects of considered applications were made as simple as possible. Both client and server applications are synchronous and based on recipes found in other chapters of this book. This allows us to compare a basic TCP client or server application with their advanced versions supporting SSL/TLS and to better understand what it takes to add SSL/TLS support to a distributed application.

Implementing the HTTP client application

HTTP clients constitute important class of distributed software and are represented by many applications. Web browsers are prominent representatives of this class. They use HTTP protocols to request web pages from web servers. However, today HTTP protocol is used not only in the web. Many distributed applications use this protocol to exchange custom data of any kind. Often, when designing a distributed application, choosing HTTP as a communication protocol is a much better idea than developing custom one.

In this recipe, we will consider an implementation of HTTP client using Boost.Asio that satisfies the following basic requirements:

▸ Supports the HTTP GET request method

▸ Executes requests asynchronously

▸ Supports request canceling

Let's move on to the implementation.

How to do it...

Because one of the requirements of our client application is to support canceling requests that have been initiated but have not been completed yet, we need to make sure that canceling is enabled on all target platforms. Therefore, we begin our client application by configuring Boost.Asio library so that request canceling is enabled. More details on issues related to asynchronous operation canceling are provided in the *Cancelling asynchronous operations* recipe in *Chapter 2, I/O Operations*:

```
#include <boost/predef.h> // Tools to identify the OS.

// We need this to enable cancelling of I/O operations on
// Windows XP, Windows Server 2003 and earlier.
// Refer to "http://www.boost.org/doc/libs/1_58_0/
// doc/html/boost_asio/reference/basic_stream_socket/
// cancel/overload1.html" for details.
#ifdef BOOST_OS_WINDOWS
#define _WIN32_WINNT 0x0501

#if _WIN32_WINNT <= 0x0502 // Windows Server 2003 or earlier.
#define BOOST_ASIO_DISABLE_IOCP
#define BOOST_ASIO_ENABLE_CANCELIO
#endif
#endif
```

Next, we include Boost.Asio library headers and also headers of some components of standard C++ libraries that we will need to implement our application:

```
#include <boost/asio.hpp>

#include <thread>
#include <mutex>
#include <memory>
#include <iostream>

using namespace boost;
```

Now, before we can jump to implementing classes and functions constituting our client application, we have to make one more preparation related to error representation and handling.

When implementing the HTTP client application, we need to deal with three classes of errors. The first class is represented by numerous errors that may occur when executing Boost.Asio functions and classes' methods. For example, if we call the `write_some()` method on an object representing a socket that has not been opened, the method will return operating system dependent error code (either by throwing an exception or by the means of an out argument depending on the method overload used), designating the fact that an invalid operation has been executed on a non-opened socket.

The second class includes both erroneous and non-erroneous statuses defined by HTTP protocol. For example, the status code 200 returned by the server as a response to particular request made by the client, designates the fact that a client's request has been fulfilled successfully. On the other hand, the status code 500 designates that while performing the requested operation, an error occurred on the server that led to the request not being fulfilled.

The third class includes errors related to the HTTP protocol itself. In case a server sends a message, as a response to correct the request made by a client and this message is not a properly structured HTTP response, the client application should have means to represent this fact in terms of error code.

Error code for the first class of errors are defined in the sources of Boost.Asio libraries. Status codes of the second class are defined by HTTP protocol. The third class is not defined anywhere and we should define corresponding error codes by ourselves in our application.

We define a single error code that represents quite a general error designating the fact that the message received from the server is not a correct HTTP response message and therefore, the client cannot parse it. Let's name this error code as `invalid_response`:

```
namespace http_errors {
  enum http_error_codes
  {
    invalid_response = 1
  };
```

Then, we define a class representing an error category, which includes the `invalid_response` error code defined above. Let's name this category as `http_errors_category`:

```cpp
class http_errors_category
  : public boost::system::error_category
{
public:
  const char* name() const BOOST_SYSTEM_NOEXCEPT
  { return "http_errors"; }

  std::string message(int e) const {
    switch (e) {
    case invalid_response:
      return "Server response cannot be parsed.";
      break;
    default:
      return "Unknown error.";
      break;
    }
  }
};
```

Then, we define a static object of this class, a function returning an instance of the object, and the overload for the `make_error_code()` function accepting error codes of our custom type `http_error_codes`:

```cpp
const boost::system::error_category&
get_http_errors_category()
{
    static http_errors_category cat;
    return cat;
}

boost::system::error_code
  make_error_code(http_error_codes e)
{
    return boost::system::error_code(
      static_cast<int>(e), get_http_errors_category());
}
} // namespace http_errors
```

The last step we need to perform before we can use our new error code in our application is to allow Boost library to *know* that the members of the `http_error_codes` enumeration should be treated as error codes. To do this, we include the following structure definition into the `boost::system` namespace:

```
namespace boost {
  namespace system {
    template<>
struct is_error_code_enum
<http_errors::http_error_codes>
{
      BOOST_STATIC_CONSTANT(bool, value = true);
    };
  } // namespace system
} // namespace boost
```

Because our HTTP client application is going to be asynchronous, the user of the client when initiating a request, will need to provide a pointer to a callback function, which will be invoked when the request completes. We need to define a type representing a pointer to such a callback function.

A callback function when called, would need to be passed arguments that clearly designate three things:

- ▸ Which request has completed
- ▸ What is the response
- ▸ Whether the request completed successfully and if not, the error code designating the error that occurred

Note that, later, we will define the `HTTPRequest` and `HTTPResponse` classes representing the HTTP request and HTTP response correspondingly, but now we use forward declarations. Here is how the callback function pointer type declaration looks:

```
class HTTPClient;
class HTTPRequest;
class HTTPResponse;

typedef void(*Callback) (const HTTPRequest& request,
  const HTTPResponse& response,
  const system::error_code& ec);
```

The HTTPResponse class

Now, we can define a class representing a HTTP response message sent to the client as a response to the request:

```cpp
class HTTPResponse {
  friend class HTTPRequest;
  HTTPResponse() :
    m_response_stream(&m_response_buf)
  {}
public:

  unsigned int get_status_code() const {
    return m_status_code;
  }

  const std::string& get_status_message() const {
    return m_status_message;
  }

  const std::map<std::string, std::string>& get_headers() {
    return m_headers;
  }

  const std::istream& get_response() const {
    return m_response_stream;
  }

private:
  asio::streambuf& get_response_buf() {
    return m_response_buf;
  }

  void set_status_code(unsigned int status_code) {
    m_status_code = status_code;
  }

  void set_status_message(const std::string& status_message) {
    m_status_message = status_message;
  }

  void add_header(const std::string& name,
  const std::string& value)
  {
    m_headers[name] = value;
```

```
    }

  private:
    unsigned int m_status_code; // HTTP status code.
    std::string m_status_message; // HTTP status message.

    // Response headers.
    std::map<std::string, std::string> m_headers;
    asio::streambuf m_response_buf;
    std::istream m_response_stream;
  };
```

The `HTTPResponse` class is quite simple. Its private data members represent parts of HTTP response such as the response status code and status message, and response headers and body. Its public interface contains methods that return the values of corresponding data members, while private methods allow setting those values.

The `HTTPRequest` class representing a HTTP request, which will be defined next, is declared as a friend to `HTTPResponse`. We will see how the objects of the `HTTPRequest` class use the private methods of the `HTTPResponse` class to set values of its data members when a response message arrives.

The HTTPRequest class

Next, we define a class representing a HTTP request containing functionality that constructs the HTTP request message based on information provided by the class user, sends it to the server, and then receives and parses the HTTP response message.

This class is at the center of our application because it contains most of its functionalities.

Later, we will define the `HTTPClient` class representing an HTTP client, responsibilities of which will be limited to maintaining a single instance of the `asio::io_service` class common to all the `HTTPRequest` objects and acting as a factory of the `HTTPRequest` objects. Therefore, we declare the `HTTPClient` class as a friend to the `HTTPRequest` class and make the `HTTPRequest` class' constructor private:

```
  class HTTPRequest {
    friend class HTTPClient;

    static const unsigned int DEFAULT_PORT = 80;

    HTTPRequest(asio::io_service& ios, unsigned int id) :
      m_port(DEFAULT_PORT),
      m_id(id),
      m_callback(nullptr),
      m_sock(ios),
```

```
      m_resolver(ios),
      m_was_cancelled(false),
      m_ios(ios)
  {}
```

The constructor accepts two arguments: a reference to an object of the `asio::io_service` class and an unsigned integer named `id`. The latter contains a unique identifier of a request, which is assigned by the user of the class and allows distinguishing request objects one from another.

Then, we define methods constituting the public interface of the class:

```cpp
public:
  void set_host(const std::string& host) {
    m_host = host;
  }

  void set_port(unsigned int port) {
    m_port = port;
  }

  void set_uri(const std::string& uri) {
    m_uri = uri;
  }

  void set_callback(Callback callback) {
    m_callback = callback;
  }

  std::string get_host() const {
    return m_host;
  }

  unsigned int get_port() const {
    return m_port;
  }

  const std::string& get_uri() const {
    return m_uri;
  }

  unsigned int get_id() const {
    return m_id;
  }
```

```cpp
void execute() {
  // Ensure that precorditions hold.
  assert(m_port > 0);
  assert(m_host.length() > 0);
  assert(m_uri.length() > 0);
  assert(m_callback != nullptr);

  // Prepare the resolving query.
  asio::ip::tcp::resolver::query resolver_query(m_host,
    std::to_string(m_port),
    asio::ip::tcp::resolver::query::numeric_service);

  std::unique_lock<std::mutex>
    cancel_lock(m_cancel_mux);

  if (m_was_cancelled) {
    cancel_lock.unlock();
    on_finish(boost::system::error_code(
    asio::error::operation_aborted));
    return;
  }

  // Resolve the host name.
  m_resolver.async_resolve(resolver_query,
    [this](const boost::system::error_code& ec,
    asio::ip::tcp::resolver::iterator iterator)
  {
    on_host_name_resolved(ec, iterator);
  });
}

void cancel() {
  std::unique_lock<std::mutex>
    cancel_lock(m_cancel_mux);

  m_was_cancelled = true;

  m_resolver.cancel();

  if (m_sock.is_open()) {
    m_sock.cancel();
  }
}
```

The public interface includes methods that allow the class' user to set and get HTTP request parameters such as the DNS name of the host running the server, protocol port number, and URI of the requested resource. Besides, there is a method that allows setting a pointer to a callback function that will be called when the request completes.

The execute() method initiates the execution of the request. Also, the cancel() method allows canceling the initiated request before it completes. We will consider how these methods work in the next section of the recipe.

Now, we define a set of private methods that contain most of the implementation details. Firstly, we define a method that is used as a callback for an asynchronous DNS name resolution operation:

```cpp
private:
  void on_host_name_resolved(
     const boost::system::error_code& ec,
     asio::ip::tcp::resolver::iterator iterator)
{
   if (ec != 0) {
     on_finish(ec);
     return;
   }

   std::unique_lock<std::mutex>
     cancel_lock(m_cancel_mux);

   if (m_was_cancelled) {
     cancel_lock.unlock();
     on_finish(boost::system::error_code(
     asio::error::operation_aborted));
     return;
   }

   // Connect to the host.
   asio::async_connect(m_sock,
     iterator,
     [this](const boost::system::error_code& ec,
     asio::ip::tcp::resolver::iterator iterator)
   {
     on_connection_established(ec, iterator);
   });

}
```

Then, we define a method used as a callback for an asynchronous connection operation, which is initiated in the on_host_name_resolved() method just defined:

```
    void on_connection_established(
      const boost::system::error_code& ec,
      asio::ip::tcp::resolver::iterator iterator)
{
      if (ec != 0) {
        on_finish(ec);
        return;
      }

      // Compose the request message.
      m_request_buf += "GET " + m_uri + " HTTP/1.1\r\n";

      // Add mandatory header.
      m_request_buf += "Host: " + m_host + "\r\n";

      m_request_buf += "\r\n";

      std::unique_lock<std::mutex>
        cancel_lock(m_cancel_mux);

      if (m_was_cancelled) {
        cancel_lock.unlock();
        on_finish(boost::system::error_code(
        asio::error::operation_aborted));
        return;
      }

      // Send the request message.
      asio::async_write(m_sock,
        asio::buffer(m_request_buf),
        [this](const boost::system::error_code& ec,
        std::size_t bytes_transferred)
      {
        on_request_sent(ec, bytes_transferred);
      });
    }
```

The next method we define—`on_request_sent()`—is a callback, which is called after the request message is sent to the server:

```
void on_request_sent(const boost::system::error_code& ec,
  std::size_t bytes_transferred)
{
  if (ec != 0) {
    on_finish(ec);
    return;
  }

  m_sock.shutdown(asio::ip::tcp::socket::shutdown_send);

  std::unique_lock<std::mutex>
    cancel_lock(m_cancel_mux);

  if (m_was_cancelled) {
    cancel_lock.unlock();
    on_finish(boost::system::error_code(
    asio::error::operation_aborted));
    return;
  }

  // Read the status line.
  asio::async_read_until(m_sock,
    m_response.get_response_buf(),
    "\r\n",
    [this](const boost::system::error_code& ec,
    std::size_t bytes_transferred)
  {
    on_status_line_received(ec, bytes_transferred);
  });
}
```

Then, we need another callback method, which is called when the first portion of the response message, namely, **status line**, is received from the server:

```
void on_status_line_received(
  const boost::system::error_code& ec,
  std::size_t bytes_transferred)
{
  if (ec != 0) {
    on_finish(ec);
```

```
    return;
  }

  // Parse the status line.
  std::string http_version;
  std::string str_status_code;
  std::string status_message;

  std::istream response_stream(
  &m_response.get_response_buf());
  response_stream >> http_version;

  if (http_version != "HTTP/1.1"){
    // Response is incorrect.
    on_finish(http_errors::invalid_response);
    return;
  }

  response_stream >> str_status_code;

  // Convert status code to integer.
  unsigned int status_code = 200;

  try {
    status_code = std::stoul(str_status_code);
  }
  catch (std::logic_error&) {
    // Response is incorrect.
    on_finish(http_errors::invalid_response);
    return;
  }

  std::getline(response_stream, status_message, '\r');
  // Remove symbol '\n' from the buffer.
  response_stream.get();

  m_response.set_status_code(status_code);
  m_response.set_status_message(status_message);

  std::unique_lock<std::mutex>
    cancel_lock(m_cancel_mux);

  if (m_was_cancelled) {
    cancel_lock.unlock();
```

```
        on_finish(boost::system::error_code(
        asio::error::operation_aborted));
        return;
    }

    // At this point the status line is successfully
    // received and parsed.
    // Now read the response headers.
    asio::async_read_until(m_sock,
        m_response.get_response_buf(),
        "\r\n\r\n",
        [this](
        const boost::system::error_code& ec,
        std::size_t bytes_transferred)
    {
        on_headers_received(ec,
            bytes_transferred);
    });
}
```

Now, we define a method that serves as a callback, which is called when the next portion of the response message—**the response headers block**—arrives from the server. We will name it as on_headers_received():

```
    void on_headers_received(const boost::system::error_code& ec,
        std::size_t bytes_transferred)
{
    if (ec != 0) {
        on_finish(ec);
        return;
    }

    // Parse and store headers.
    std::string header, header_name, header_value;
    std::istream response_stream(
    &m_response.get_response_buf());

    while (true) {
        std::getline(response_stream, header, '\r');

        // Remove \n symbol from the stream.
        response_stream.get();
```

```cpp
    if (header == "")
      break;

    size_t separator_pos = header.find(':');
    if (separator_pos != std::string::npos) {
      header_name = header.substr(0,
      separator_pos);

      if (separator_pos < header.length() - 1)
        header_value =
        header.substr(separator_pos + 1);
      else
        header_value = "";

      m_response.add_header(header_name,
      header_value);
    }
  }

  std::unique_lock<std::mutex>
    cancel_lock(m_cancel_mux);

  if (m_was_cancelled) {
    cancel_lock.unlock();
    on_finish(boost::system::error_code(
    asio::error::operation_aborted));
    return;
  }

  // Now we want to read the response body.
  asio::async_read(m_sock,
    m_response.get_response_buf(),
    [this](
    const boost::system::error_code& ec,
    std::size_t bytes_transferred)
  {
    on_response_body_received(ec,
      bytes_transferred);
  });

  return;
}
```

Besides, we need a method that will handle the last part of the response—**the response body**. The following method is used as a callback, which is called after the response body arrives from the server:

```cpp
void on_response_body_received(
const boost::system::error_code& ec,
    std::size_t bytes_transferred)
{
    if (ec == asio::error::eof)
      on_finish(boost::system::error_code());
    else
      on_finish(ec);
}
```

Finally, we define the `on_finish()` method that serves as a final point of all execution paths (including erroneous) that start in the `execute()` method. This method is called when the request completes (either successfully or not) and its purpose is to call the callback provided by the `HTTPRequest` class' user to notify it about the completion of the request:

```cpp
void on_finish(const boost::system::error_code& ec)
{
    if (ec != 0) {
      std::cout << "Error occured! Error code = "
        << ec.value()
        << ". Message: " << ec.message();
    }

    m_callback(*this, m_response, ec);

    return;
}
```

We will need some data fields associated with each instance of the `HTTPRequest` class. Here, we declare the class' corresponding data members:

```cpp
private:
  // Request parameters.
  std::string m_host;
  unsigned int m_port;
  std::string m_uri;

  // Object unique identifier.
  unsigned int m_id;
```

```
// Callback to be called when request completes.
Callback m_callback;

// Buffer containing the request line.
std::string m_request_buf;

asio::ip::tcp::socket m_sock;
asio::ip::tcp::resolver m_resolver;

HTTPResponse m_response;

bool m_was_cancelled;
std::mutex m_cancel_mux;

asio::io_service& m_ios;
```

The last thing to add is the closing bracket to designate the end of the HTTPRequest class definition:

```
};
```

The HTTPClient class

The last class that we need in our application is the one that would be responsible for the following three functions:

▸ To establish a threading policy

▸ To spawn and destroy threads in a pool of threads running the Boost.Asio event loop and delivering asynchronous operations' completion events

▸ To act as a factory of the HTTPRequest objects

We will name this class as HTTPClient:

```
class HTTPClient {
public:
  HTTPClient(){
    m_work.reset(new boost::asio::io_service::work(m_ios));

    m_thread.reset(new std::thread([this](){
      m_ios.run();
    }));
  }

  std::shared_ptr<HTTPRequest>
  create_request(unsigned int id)
  {
```

```
    return std::shared_ptr<HTTPRequest>(
    new HTTPRequest(m_ios, id));
  }

  void close() {
    // Destroy the work object.
    m_work.reset(NULL);

    // Waiting for the I/O thread to exit.
    m_thread->join();
  }

private:
  asio::io_service m_ios;
  std::unique_ptr<boost::asio::io_service::work> m_work;
  std::unique_ptr<std::thread> m_thread;
};
```

The callback and the main() entry point function

At this point, we have the basic HTTP client that comprises three classes and several supplementary data types. Now we will define two functions that are not parts of the client, but demonstrate how to use it to communicate with the server using the HTTP protocol. The first function will be used as a callback, which will be called when the request completes. Its signature must correspond to the function pointer type `Callback` defined earlier. Let's name our callback function as `handler()`:

```
void handler(const HTTPRequest& request,
  const HTTPResponse& response,
  const system::error_code& ec)
{
  if (ec == 0) {
    std::cout << "Request #" << request.get_id()
      << " has completed. Response: "
      << response.get_response().rdbuf();
  }
  else if (ec == asio::error::operation_aborted) {
    std::cout << "Request #" << request.get_id()
      << " has been cancelled by the user."
      << std::endl;
  }
  else {
    std::cout << "Request #" << request.get_id()
      << " failed! Error code = " << ec.value()
      << ". Error message = " << ec.message()
```

```
        << std::endl;
  }

  return;
}
```

The second and the last function we need to define is the `main()` application entry point function that uses the HTTP client to send HTTP requests to the server:

```cpp
int main()
{
  try {
    HTTPClient client;

    std::shared_ptr<HTTPRequest> request_one =
      client.create_request(1);

    request_one->set_host("localhost");
    request_one->set_uri("/index.html");
    request_one->set_port(3333);
    request_one->set_callback(handler);

    request_one->execute();

    std::shared_ptr<HTTPRequest> request_two =
      client.create_request(1);

    request_two->set_host("localhost");
    request_two->set_uri("/example.html");
    request_two->set_port(3333);
    request_two->set_callback(handler);

    request_two->execute();

    request_two->cancel();

    // Do nothing for 15 seconds, letting the
    // request complete.
    std::this_thread::sleep_for(std::chrono::seconds(15));

    // Closing the client and exiting the application.
    client.close();
  }
```

```
    catch (system::system_error &e) {
      std::cout << "Error occured! Error code = " << e.code()
        << ". Message: " << e.what();

      return e.code().value();
    }

    return 0;
  };
```

How it works...

Now let's consider how our HTTP client works. The application consists of five components, among which are the three classes such as `HTTPClient`, `HTTPRequest`, and `HTTPResponse`, and two functions such as the `handler()` callback function and the `main()` application entry point function. Let's consider how each component works separately.

The HTTPClient class

A class' constructor begins with creating an instance of the `asio::io_service::work` object in order to make sure that threads running the event loop do not exit this loop when there are no pending asynchronous operations. Then, a thread of control is spawned and added to the pool by calling the `run()` method on the `m_ios` object. This is where the `HTTPClient` class performs its first and part of the second functions, namely, establishing threading policy and adding threads to the pool.

The third function of the `HTTPClient` class—to act as a factory of the object representing HTTP requests—is performed in its `create_request()` public method. This method creates an instance of the `HTTPRequest` class in the free memory and returns a shared pointer object pointing to it. As its input argument, the method accepts an integer value that represents the unique identifier to be assigned to the newly created request object. This identifier is used to distinguish between different request objects.

The `close()` method from the class' public interface destroys the `asio::io_service::work` object, allowing threads to exit the event loop just as soon as all pending operations complete. The method blocks until all threads exit.

The HTTPRequest class

Let's begin considering the `HTTPRequest` class' behavior by inspecting its data members and their purpose. The `HTTPRequest` class contains 12 data members, among which are the following:

▶ Request parameters:

```
std::string m_host;
unsigned int m_port;
std::string m_uri;
```

▶ A unique identifier of the request:

```
unsigned int m_id;
```

▶ A pointer to the callback function provided by the class' user to be called when a request completes:

```
Callback m_callback;
```

▶ A string buffer used to store the HTTP request message:

```
std::string m_request_buf;
```

▶ A socket object used to communicate with the server:

```
asio::ip::tcp::socket m_sock;
```

▶ A resolver object used to resolve the DNS name of the server host provided by the user:

```
asio::ip::tcp::resolver m_resolver;
```

▶ An instance of the `HTTPResponse` class that represents the response received from the server:

```
HTTPResponse m_response;
```

▶ A boolean flag and a `mutex` object supporting the request canceling functionality (which will be explained later):

```
bool m_was_cancelled;
std::mutex m_cancel_mux;
```

▶ Also, a reference to an instance of the `asio::io_service` class required by resolver and socket objects. The single instance of the `asio::io_service` class is maintained by an object of the `HTTPClient` class:

```
asio::io_service& m_ios;
```

An instance of the HTTPRequest object represents a single HTTP GET request. The class is designed so that in order to send a request, two steps need to be performed. Firstly, the parameters of the request and the callback function to be called when the request completes are set by calling the corresponding setter methods on the object. Then, as a second step, the execute() method is invoked to initiate the request execution. When the request completes, the callback function is called.

The set_host(), set_port(), set_uri(), and set_callback() setter methods allow setting a server host DNS name and port number, URI of the requested resource, and a callback function to be called when the request completes. Each of these methods accepts one argument and stores its value in the corresponding HTTPRequest object's data member.

The get_host(), get_port(), and get_uri() getter methods return values set by corresponding setter methods. The get_id() getter method returns a request object's unique identifier, which is passed to the object's constructor on instantiation.

The execute() method begins the execution of a request by initiating a sequence of asynchronous operations. Each asynchronous operation performs one step of request execution procedure.

Because a server host in the request object is represented with a DNS name (rather than with an IP address), before sending the request message to the server, the specified DNS name must be resolved and transformed into an IP address. Therefore, the first step in the request execution is DNS name resolution. The execute() method begins with preparing the resolving query and then calls the resolver object's async_resolve() method, specifying the HTTPRequest class' on_host_name_resolve() private method as an operation completion callback.

When the server host DNS name is resolved, the on_host_name_resolved() method is called. This method is passed two arguments: the first of which is an error code, designating the status of the operation, and the second one is the iterator that can be used to iterate through a list of endpoints resulting from a resolution process.

The on_host_name_resolved() method initiates the next asynchronous operation in a sequence, namely socket connection, by calling asio::async_connect() free function passing socket object m_sock and iterator parameter to it so that it connects the socket to the first valid endpoint. The on_connection_established() method is specified as an asynchronous connection operation completion callback.

When an asynchronous connection operation completes, the on_connection_established() method is invoked. The first argument passed to it is named ec that designates the operation completion status. If its value is equal to zero, it means that the socket was successfully connected to one of the endpoints. The on_connection_established() method constructs the HTTP GET request message using request parameters stored in the corresponding data members of the HTTPRequest object. Then, the asio::async_write() free function is called to asynchronously send a constructed HTTP request message to the server. The class' private method on_request_sent() is specified as a callback to be called when the asio::async_write() operation completes.

After a request is sent, and if it is sent successfully, the client application has to let the server know that the full request is sent and the client is not going to send anything else by shutting down the send part of the socket. Then, the client has to wait for the response message from the server. And this is what the `on_request_sent()` method does. Firstly, it calls the socket object's `shutdown()` method, specifying that the send part should be closed by the passing value `asio::ip::tcp::socket::shutdown_send` to the method as an argument. Then, it calls the `asio::async_read_until()` free function to receive a response from the server.

Because the response may be potentially very big and we do not know its size beforehand, we do not want to read it all at once. We first want to read the **HTTP response status line** only; then, having analyzed it, either continue reading the rest of the response (if we think we need it) or discard it. Therefore, we pass the `\r\n` symbols sequence, designating the end of the HTTP response status line as a delimiter argument to the `asio::async_read_until()` method. The `on_status_line_received()` method is specified as an operation completion callback.

When the status line is received, the `on_status_line_received()` method is invoked. This method performs parsing of the status line, extracting values designating the HTTP protocol version, response status code, and response status message from it. Each value is analyzed for correctness. We expect the HTTP version to be 1.1, otherwise the response is considered incorrect and the request execution is interrupted. The status code should be an integer value. If the string-to-integer conversion fails, the response is considered incorrect and its further processing is interrupted too. If the response status line is correct, the request execution continues. The extracted status code and status message are stored in the `m_response` member object, and the next asynchronous operation in the request execution operation sequence is initiated. Now, we want to read the response headers block.

According to the HTTP protocol, the response headers block ends with the `\r\n\r\n` symbols sequence. Therefore, in order to read it, we call the `asio::async_read_until()` free function one more time, specifying the string `\r\n\r\n` as a delimiter. The `on_headers_received()` method is specified as a callback.

When the response headers block is received, the `on_headers_received()` method is invoked. In this method, the response headers block is parsed and broken into separate name-value pairs and stored in the `m_response` member object as a part of the response.

Having received and parsed the headers, we want to read the last part of the response—the response body. To do this, an asynchronous reading operation is initiated by calling the `asio::async_read()` free function. The `on_response_body_received()` method is specified as a callback.

Eventually, the `on_response_body_received()` method is invoked notifying us of the fact that the whole response message has been received. Because the HTTP server may shutdown the send part of its socket just after it sends the last part of the response message, on the client side, the last reading operation may complete with an error code equal to the `asio::error::eof` value. This should not be treated as an actual error, but rather as a normal event. Therefore, if the `on_response_body_received()` method is called with the `ec` argument equal to `asio::error::eof`, we pass the default constructed object of the `boost::system::error_code` class to the `on_finish()` method in order to designate that the request execution is completed successfully. Otherwise, the `on_finish()` method is called with an argument representing the original error code. The `on_finish()` method in its turn calls the callback provided by the client of the `HTTPRequest` class object.

When the callback returns, request processing is considered finished.

The HTTPResponse class

The `HTTPResponse` class does not provide much functionality. It is more like a plain data structure containing data members representing different parts of a response, with getter and setter methods defined, allowing getting and setting corresponding data member values.

All setter methods are private and only the objects of the `HTTPRequest` class has access to them (recall that the `HTTPRequest` class is declared as the `HTTPResponse` class' friend). Each object of the `HTTPRequest` class has a data member that is an instance of the `HTTPResponse` class. The object of the `HTTPRequest` class sets values of its member object of `HTTPResponse` class as it receives and parses the response received from a HTTP server.

Callback and the main() entry point functions

These functions demonstrate how to use the `HTTPClient` and `HTTPRequest` classes in order to send the `GET` HTTP requests to the HTTP server and then how to use the `HTTPResponse` class to obtain the response.

The `main()` function first creates an instance of the `HTTPClient` class and then uses it to create two instances of the `HTTPRequest` class, each representing a separate `GET` HTTP request. Both request objects are provided with request parameters and then executed. However, just after the second request has been executed, the first one is canceled by invoking its `cancel()` method.

The `handler()` function, which is used as a completion callback for both request objects created in the `main()` function, is invoked when each request completes regardless of whether it succeeded, failed, or was canceled. The `handler()` function analyses the error code and the request and response objects passed to it as arguments and output corresponding messages to the standard output stream.

See also

▸ The *Implementing asynchronous TCP client* recipe from *Chapter 3, Implementing Client Applications*, provides more information on how to implement an asynchronous TCP client.

▸ The *Using timers* recipe from *Chapter 6, Other Topics*, demonstrates how to use timers provided by Boost.Asio. Timers can be used to implement an asynchronous operation timeout mechanism.

Implementing the HTTP server application

Nowadays, there are plenty of HTTP server applications available in the market. However, sometimes there is a need to implement a custom one. This could be a small and simple server, supporting a specific subset of HTTP protocol possibly with custom extensions, or maybe not an HTTP server but a server supporting a communication protocol, which is similar to HTTP or is based on it.

In this recipe, we will consider the implementation of basic HTTP server application using Boost.Asio. Here is the set of requirements that our application must satisfy:

▸ It should support the HTTP 1.1 protocol

▸ It should support the GET method

▸ It should be able to process multiple requests in parallel, that is, it should be an asynchronous parallel server

In fact, we have already considered the implementation of the server application that partially fulfils specified requirements. In *Chapter 4, Implementing Server Applications*, the recipe named *Implementing an asynchronous TCP server* demonstrates how to implement an asynchronous parallel TCP server, which communicates with clients according to a dummy application layer protocol. All the communication functionality and protocol details are encapsulated in a single class named Service. All other classes and functions defined in that recipe are infrastructural in their purpose and isolated from the protocol details. Therefore, the current recipe will be based on the one from *Chapter 4, Implementing Server Applications*, and here we will only consider the implementation of the Service class as all other components stay the same.

> Note that, in this recipe, we do not consider the security aspect of the application. Make sure the server is protected before making it available to the public, where though operating correctly and in accordance with HTTP protocol, it could be compromised by the culprits due to security breaches.

Now let's move on to the implementation of the HTTP server application.

Getting ready...

Because the application demonstrated in this recipe is based on other applications demonstrated in the recipe named *Implementing asynchronous TCP server* from *Chapter 4, Implementing Server Applications*, it is necessary to get acquainted with that recipe before proceeding with this one.

How to do it...

We begin our application by including header files containing declarations and definitions of data types and functions that we will use:

```
#include <boost/asio.hpp>
#include <boost/filesystem.hpp>

#include <fstream>
#include <atomic>
#include <thread>
#include <iostream>

using namespace boost;
```

Next, we start defining the `Service` class that provides the implementation of the HTTP protocol. Firstly, we declare a static constant table containing HTTP status codes and status messages. The definition of the table will be given after the `Service` class' definition:

```
class Service {
   static const std::map<unsigned int, std::string>
http_status_table;
```

The class' constructor accepts a single parameter—shared pointer pointing to an instance of a socket connected to a client. Here's the definition of the constructor:

```
public:
  Service(std::shared_ptr<boost::asio::ip::tcp::socket> sock) :
    m_sock(sock),
    m_request(4096),
    m_response_status_code(200), // Assume success.
    m_resource_size_bytes(0)
  {};
```

Next, we define a single method constituting the `Service` class' public interface. This method initiates an asynchronous communication session with the client connected to the socket, pointer to which was passed to the `Service` class' constructor:

```
void start_handling() {
  asio::async_read_until(*m_sock.get(),
    m_request,
    "\r\n",
    [this](
    const boost::system::error_code& ec,
    std::size_t bytes_transferred)
  {
    on_request_line_received(ec,
      bytes_transferred);
  });
}
```

Then, we define a set of private methods that perform receiving and processing of the request sent by the client, parse and execute the request, and send the response back. Firstly, we define a method that processes the **HTTP request line**:

```
private:
  void on_request_line_received(
    const boost::system::error_code& ec,
    std::size_t bytes_transferred)
  {
    if (ec != 0) {
      std::cout << "Error occured! Error code = "
        << ec.value()
        << ". Message: " << ec.message();

      if (ec == asio::error::not_found) {
        // No delimiter has been found in the
        // request message.

        m_response_status_code = 413;
        send_response();

        return;
      }
      else {
        // In case of any other error -
        // close the socket and clean up.
        on_finish();
        return;
```

```
    }
  }

  // Parse the request line.
  std::string request_line;
  std::istream request_stream(&m_request);
  std::getline(request_stream, request_line, '\r');
  // Remove symbol '\n' from the buffer.
  request_stream.get();

  // Parse the request line.
  std::string request_method;
  std::istringstream request_line_stream(request_line);
  request_line_stream >> request_method;

  // We only support GET method.
  if (request_method.compare("GET") != 0) {
    // Unsupported method.
    m_response_status_code = 501;
    send_response();

    return;
  }

  request_line_stream >> m_requested_resource;

  std::string request_http_version;
  request_line_stream >> request_http_version;

  if (request_http_version.compare("HTTP/1.1") != 0) {
    // Unsupported HTTP version or bad request.
    m_response_status_code = 505;
    send_response();

    return;
  }

  // At this point the request line is successfully
  // received and parsed. Now read the request headers.
  asio::async_read_until(*m_sock.get(),
    m_request,
    "\r\n\r\n",
    [this](
    const boost::system::error_code& ec,
```

```
    std::size_t bytes_transferred)
  {
    on_headers_received(ec,
      bytes_transferred);
  });

  return;
}
```

Next, we define a method intended to process and store the **request headers block**, containing the request headers:

```
void on_headers_received(const boost::system::error_code& ec,
  std::size_t bytes_transferred)
{
  if (ec != 0) {
    std::cout << "Error occured! Error code = "
      << ec.value()
      << ". Message: " << ec.message();

    if (ec == asio::error::not_found) {
      // No delimiter has been fonud in the
      // request message.

      m_response_status_code = 413;
      send_response();
      return;
    }
    else {
      // In case of any other error - close the
      // socket and clean up.
      on_finish();
      return;
    }
  }

  // Parse and store headers.
  std::istream request_stream(&m_request);
  std::string header_name, header_value;

  while (!request_stream.eof()) {
    std::getline(request_stream, header_name, ':');
    if (!request_stream.eof()) {
      std::getline(request_stream,
        header_value,
```

```
'\r');

    // Remove symbol \n from the stream.
    request_stream.get();
    m_request_headers[header_name] =
    header_value;
  }
}

// Now we have all we need to process the request.
process_request();
send_response();

return;
}
```

Besides, we need a method that can perform the actions needed to fulfill the request sent by the client. We define the `process_request()` method, whose purpose is to read the contents of the requested resource from the file system and store it in the buffer, ready to be sent back to the client:

```
void process_request() {
  // Read file.
  std::string resource_file_path =
  std::string("D:\\http_root") +
  m_requested_resource;

  if (!boost::filesystem::exists(resource_file_path)) {
    // Resource not found.
    m_response_status_code = 404;

    return;
  }

  std::ifstream resource_fstream(
  resource_file_path,
  std::ifstream::binary);

  if (!resource_fstream.is_open()) {
    // Could not open file.
    // Something bad has happened.
    m_response_status_code = 500;
```

```
      return;
  }


  // Find out file size.
  resource_fstream.seekg(0, std::ifstream::end);
  m_resource_size_bytes =
  static_cast<std::size_t>(
  resource_fstream.tellg());

  m_resource_buffer.reset(
  new char[m_resource_size_bytes]);

  resource_fstream.seekg(std::ifstream::beg);
  resource_fstream.read(m_resource_buffer.get(),
  m_resource_size_bytes);

  m_response_headers += std::string("content-length") +
    ": " +
    std::to_string(m_resource_size_bytes) +
    "\r\n";
  }
```

Finally, we define a method that composes a response message and send it to the client:

```
void send_response() {
  m_sock->shutdown(
  asio::ip::tcp::socket::shutdown_receive);

  auto status_line =
    http_status_table.at(m_response_status_code);

  m_response_status_line = std::string("HTTP/1.1 ") +
    status_line +
    "\r\n";

  m_response_headers += "\r\n";

  std::vector<asio::const_buffer> response_buffers;
  response_buffers.push_back(
  asio::buffer(m_response_status_line));
```

```
    if (m_response_headers.length() > 0) {
      response_buffers.push_back(
      asio::buffer(m_response_headers));
    }

    if (m_resource_size_bytes > 0) {
      response_buffers.push_back(
      asio::buffer(m_resource_buffer.get(),
      m_resource_size_bytes));
    }

    // Initiate asynchronous write operation.
    asio::async_write(*m_sock.get(),
      response_buffers,
      [this](
      const boost::system::error_code& ec,
      std::size_t bytes_transferred)
    {
      on_response_sent(ec,
        bytes_transferred);
    });
  }
```

When the response sending is complete, we need to shut down the socket to let the client know that a full response has been sent and no more data will be sent by the server. We define the `on_response_sent()` method for this purpose:

```
    void on_response_sent(const boost::system::error_code& ec,
      std::size_t bytes_transferred)
  {
    if (ec != 0) {
      std::cout << "Error occured! Error code = "
        << ec.value()
        << ". Message: " << ec.message();
    }

    m_sock->shutdown(asio::ip::tcp::socket::shutdown_both);

    on_finish();
  }
```

The last method we need to define is the one that performs cleanup and deletes an instance of the `Service` object, when the communication session is finished and the object is not needed anymore is not needed anymore:

```
// Here we perform the cleanup.
void on_finish() {
  delete this;
}
```

Of course, we will need some data members in our class. We declare the following data members:

```
private:
  std::shared_ptr<boost::asio::ip::tcp::socket> m_sock;
  boost::asio::streambuf m_request;
  std::map<std::string, std::string> m_request_headers;
  std::string m_requested_resource;

  std::unique_ptr<char[]> m_resource_buffer;
  unsigned int m_response_status_code;
  std::size_t m_resource_size_bytes;
  std::string m_response_headers;
  std::string m_response_status_line;
};
```

The last thing we need to do to complete the definition of the class representing a service is to define the `http_status_table` static member declared before and fill it with data—HTTP status code and corresponding status messages:

```
const std::map<unsigned int, std::string>
  Service::http_status_table =
{
  { 200, "200 OK" },
  { 404, "404 Not Found" },
  { 413, "413 Request Entity Too Large" },
  { 500, "500 Server Error" },
  { 501, "501 Not Implemented" },
  { 505, "505 HTTP Version Not Supported" }
};
```

Our `Service` class is now ready.

How it works...

Let's begin with considering the `Service` class' data members and then switch to its functionality. The `Service` class contains the following non-static data members:

- `std::shared_ptr<boost::asio::ip::tcp::socket> m_sock`: This is a shared pointer to a TCP socket object connected to the client

- `boost::asio::streambuf m_request`: This is a buffer into which the request message is read

- `std::map<std::string, std::string> m_request_headers`: This is a map where request headers are put when the HTTP request headers block is parsed

- `std::string m_requested_resource`: This is the URI of the resource requested by the client

- `std::unique_ptr<char[]> m_resource_buffer`: This is a buffer where the contents of a requested resource is stored before being sent to the client as a part of the response message

- `unsigned int m_response_status_code`: This is the HTTP response status code

- `std::size_t m_resource_size_bytes`: This is the size of the contents of the requested resource

- `std::string m_response_headers`: This is a string containing a properly formatted response headers block

- `std::string m_response_status_line`: This contains a response status line

Now that we know the purpose of the `Service` class' data members, let's trace how it works. Here, we will only consider how the `Service` class works. The description of all other components of the server application and how they work is given in the recipe named *Implementing an asynchronous TCP server* in *Chapter 4, Implementing Server Applications*.

When a client sends a TCP connection request and this request is accepted on the server (this happens in the `Acceptor` class, which is not considered in this recipe), an instance of the `Service` class is created and its constructor is passed a shared pointer pointing to the TCP socket object, connected to that client. The pointer to the socket is stored in the `Service` object's data member `m_sock`.

Besides, during the construction of the `Service` object, the `m_request` stream buffer member is initialized with the value of 4096, which sets the maximum size of the buffer in bytes. Limiting the size of the request buffer is a security measure, which helps to protect the server from malicious clients that may try to send very long dummy request messages exhausting all memory at the disposal of the server application. For the correct request, a buffer of 4096 bytes in size is more than enough.

After an instance of the `Service` class has been constructed, its `start_handling()` method is called by the `Acceptor` class. From this method, the sequence of asynchronous method invocations begins, which performs request receiving, processing, and response sending. The `start_handling()` method immediately initiates an asynchronous reading operation calling the `asio::async_read_until()` function in order to receive the HTTP request line sent by the client. The `on_request_line_received()` method is specified as a callback.

When the `on_request_line_received()` method is invoked, we first check the error code specifying the operation completion status. If the status code is not equal to zero, we consider two options. The first option—when the error code is equal to the `asio::error::not_found` value—means that more bytes have been received from the client than the size of the buffer and the delimiter of the HTTP request line (the `\r\n` symbol sequence) has not been encountered. This case is described by the HTTP status code 413. We set the value of the `m_response_status_code` member variable to 413 and call the `send_response()` method that initiates the operation that sends a response designating the error back to the client. We will consider the `send_response()` method later in this section. At this point, the request processing is finished.

If the error code neither designates success nor is equal to `asio::error::not_found`, it means that some other error has occurred from which we cannot recover, therefore, we just output the information about the error and do not reply to the client at all. The `on_finish()` method is called to perform the cleanup, and the communication with the client is interrupted.

Finally, if receiving of the HTTP request line succeeds, it is parsed to extract the HTTP request method, the URI identifying the requested resource and the HTTP protocol version. Because our sample server only supports the `GET` method, if the method specified in the request line is different from `GET`, further request processing is interrupted and the response containing the error code 501 is sent to the client to inform it that the method specified in the request is not supported by the server.

Likewise, the HTTP protocol version specified by the client in the HTTP request line is checked to be the one supported by the server. Because our server application supports only version 1.1, if the version specified by the client is different, the response with the HTTP status code 505 is sent to the client and the request processing is interrupted.

A URI string extracted from the HTTP request line is stored in the `m_requested_resource` data member and will be used later.

When the HTTP request line is received and parsed, we continue reading the request message in order to read the request headers block. To do this, the `asio::async_read_until()` function is called. Because the request headers block ends with the `\r\n\r\n` symbol sequence, this symbol sequence is passed to the function as a delimiter argument. The `on_headers_received()` method is specified as an operation completion callback.

The `on_headers_received()` method performs error checking similar to the one that is performed in the `on_request_line_received()` method. In case of an error, request processing interrupts. In the case of success, the HTTP request headers block is parsed and broken into separate name-value pairs, which are then stored in the `m_request_headers` member map. After the headers block has been parsed, the `process_request()` and `send_response()` methods are called consequently.

The purpose of the `process_request()` method is to read the file specified in the request as the URI and put its content to the buffer, from which the contents will be sent to the client as a part of the response message. If the specified file is not found in the server root directory, the HTTP status code 404 (page not found) code is sent to the client as a part of the response message and the request processing interrupts.

However, if the requested file is found, its size is first calculated and then the buffer of the corresponding size is allocated in the free memory and the file contents are read in that buffer.

After this, an HTTP header named *content-length* specifying the size of the response body is added to the `m_response_headers` string data member. This data member represents the response headers block and its value will later be used as a part of the response message.

At this point, all ingredients required to construct the HTTP response message are available and we can move on to preparing and sending the response to the client. This is done in the `send_response()` method.

The `send_response()` method starts with shutting down the receive side of the socket letting the client know that the server will not read any data from it anymore. Then, it extracts the response status message corresponding to the status code stored in the `m_response_status_code` member variable from the `http_status_table` static table.

Next, the HTTP response status line is constructed and the headers block is appended with the delimiting symbol sequence `\r\n` according to the HTTP protocol. At this point, all the components of the response message—the response status line, response headers block, and response body—are ready to be sent to the client. The components are combined in the form of a vector of buffers, each represented with an instance of the `asio::const_buffer` class and containing one component of the response message. A vector of buffers embodies a composite buffer consisting of three parts. When this composite buffer is constructed, it is passed to the `asio::async_write()` function to be sent to the client. The `Service` class' `on_response_sent()` method is specified as a callback.

When the response message is sent and the `on_response_sent()` callback method is invoked, it first checks the error code and outputs the log message if the operation fails; then, it shuts down the socket and calls the `on_finish()` method. The `on_finish()` method in its turn deletes the instance of the `Service` object in the context of which it is called.

At this point, client handling is finished.

See also

▶ The *Implementing an asynchronous TCP server* recipe from *Chapter 4, Implementing Server Applications*, provides more information on how to implement the asynchronous TCP server used as a base for this recipe.

▶ The *Using timers* recipe from *Chapter 6, Other Topics*, demonstrates how to use timers provided by Boost.Asio. Timers can be used to implement an asynchronous operation timeout mechanism.

Adding SSL/TLS support to client applications

Client applications usually use SSL/TLS protocol to send sensitive data such as passwords, credit card numbers, personal data. SSL/TLS protocol allows clients to authenticate the server and encrypt the data. The authentication of the server allows the client to make sure that the data will be sent to the expected addressee (and not to a malicious one). Data encryption guarantees that even if the transmitted data is intercepted somewhere on its way to the server, the interceptor will not be able to use it.

This recipe demonstrates how to implement a synchronous TCP client application supporting SSL/TLS protocol using the Boost.Asio and OpenSSL libraries. The TCP client application demonstrated in the recipe named *Implementing synchronous TCP client* from *Chapter 3, Implementing Client Applications*, is taken as a base for this recipe, and some code changes and additions are made to it in order to add support for SSL/TLS protocol. The code that differs from that of the base implementation of the synchronous TCP client is *highlighted* so that the code directly related to SSL/TLS support is better distinguished from the rest of the code.

Getting ready...

Before setting out to this recipe, OpenSSL library must be installed and the project must be linked against it. Procedures related to the installation of the library or linking the project against it are beyond the scope of this book. Refer to the OpenSSL library documentation for more information.

Besides, because this recipe is based on another recipe named *Implementing a synchronous TCP Client* from *Chapter 3, Implementing Client Applications*, it is highly advised to get acquainted with it before proceeding to this one.

How to do it...

The following code sample demonstrates the possible implementation of a synchronous TCP client application supporting SSL/TLS protocol to authenticate the server and encrypt the data being transmitted.

We begin our application by adding the `include` and `using` directives:

```
#include <boost/asio.hpp>
#include <boost/asio/ssl.hpp>
#include <iostream>

using namespace boost;
```

The `<boost/asio/ssl.hpp>` header contains types and functions providing integration with OpenSSL library.

Next, we define a class that plays the role of the synchronous SSL/TLS-enabled TCP client:

```
class SyncSSLClient {
public:
  SyncSSLClient(const std::string& raw_ip_address,
    unsigned short port_num) :
    m_ep(asio::ip::address::from_string(raw_ip_address),
    port_num),
    m_ssl_context(asio::ssl::context::sslv3_client),
    m_ssl_stream(m_ios, m_ssl_context)
  {
    // Set verification mode and designate that
    // we want to perform verification.
    m_ssl_stream.set_verify_mode(asio::ssl::verify_peer);

    // Set verification callback.
    m_ssl_stream.set_verify_callback([this](
      bool preverified,
      asio::ssl::verify_context& context)->bool{
      return on_peer_verify(preverified, context);
    });
  }

  void connect() {
    // Connect the TCP socket.
    m_ssl_stream.lowest_layer().connect(m_ep);
```

```
    // Perform the SSL handshake.
    m_ssl_stream.handshake(asio::ssl::stream_base::client);
  }

  void close() {
    // We ignore any errors that might occur
    // during shutdown as we anyway can't
    // do anything about them.
    boost::system::error_code ec;

    m_ssl_stream.shutdown(ec); // Shutdown SSL.

    // Shut down the socket.
    m_ssl_stream.lowest_layer().shutdown(
      boost::asio::ip::tcp::socket::shutdown_both, ec);

    m_ssl_stream.lowest_layer().close(ec);
  }

  std::string emulate_long_computation_op(
    unsigned int duration_sec) {

    std::string request = "EMULATE_LONG_COMP_OP "
      + std::to_string(duration_sec)
      + "\n";

    send_request(request);
    return receive_response();
  };

private:
  bool on_peer_verify(bool preverified,
    asio::ssl::verify_context& context)
  {
    // Here the certificate should be verified and the
    // verification result should be returned.
    return true;
  }

  void send_request(const std::string& request) {
    asio::write(m_ssl_stream, asio::buffer(request));
  }
```

```
    std::string receive_response() {
      asio::streambuf buf;
      asio::read_until(m_ssl_stream, buf, '\n');

      std::string response;
      std::istream input(&buf);
      std::getline(input, response);

      return response;
    }

  private:
    asio::io_service m_ios;
    asio::ip::tcp::endpoint m_ep;

    asio::ssl::context m_ssl_context;
    asio::ssl::stream<asio::ip::tcp::socket>m_ssl_stream;
};
```

Now we implement the `main()` application entry point function that uses the
`SyncSSLClient` class to authenticate the server and securely communicate with
it using SSL/TLS protocol:

```
int main()
{
  const std::string raw_ip_address = "127.0.0.1";
  const unsigned short port_num = 3333;

  try {
    SyncSSLClient client(raw_ip_address, port_num);

    // Sync connect.
    client.connect();

    std::cout << "Sending request to the server... "
      << std::endl;

    std::string response =
      client.emulate_long_computation_op(10);

    std::cout << "Response received: " << response
      << std::endl;
```

```
    // Close the connection and free resources.
    client.close();
  }
  catch (system::system_error &e) {
    std::cout << "Error occured! Error code = " << e.code()
      << ". Message: " << e.what();

    return e.code().value();
  }

  return 0;
}
```

How it works...

The sample client application consists of two main components: the SyncSSLClient class and a main() application entry point function that uses the SyncSSLClient class to communicate with the server application over SSL/TLS protocol. Let's consider how each component works separately.

The SyncSSLClient class

The SyncSSLClient class is the key component in our application. It implements the communication functionality.

The class has four private data members as follows:

- asio::io_service m_ios: This is an object providing access to the operating system's communication services that are used by the socket object.

- asio::ip::tcp::endpoint m_ep: This is an endpoint designating the server application.

- asio::ssl::context m_ssl_context: This is an object representing SSL context; basically, this is a wrapper around the SSL_CTX data structure defined by OpenSSL library. This object contains global settings and parameters used by other objects and functions involved in the process of communication using SSL/TLS protocol.

- asio::ssl::stream<asio::ip::tcp::socket> m_ssl_stream: This represents a stream that wraps a TCP socket object and implements all SSL/TLS communication operations.

Each object of the class is intended to communicate with a single server. Therefore, the class' constructor accepts an IP address and a protocol port number designating the server application as its input arguments. These values are used to instantiate the m_ep data member in the constructor's initialization list.

Next, the `m_ssl_context` and `m_ssl_stream` members of the `SyncSSLClient` class are instantiated. We pass the `asio::ssl::context::sslv23_client` value to the `m_ssl_context` object's constructor to designate that the context will be used by the application playing a role of a *client* only and that we want to support multiple secure protocols including multiple versions of SSL and TLS. This value defined by Boost.Asio corresponds to a value representing a connection method returned by the `SSLv23_client_method()` function defined by OpenSSL library.

The SSL stream object `m_ssl_stream` is set up in the `SyncSSLClient` class' constructor. Firstly, the peer verification mode is set to `asio::ssl::verify_peer`, which means that we want to perform peer verification during a handshake. Then, we set a verification callback method that will be called when certificates arrive from the server. The callback is invoked once for each certificate in the certificates chain sent by the server.

The class' `on_peer_verify()` method that is set as a peer verification callback is a dummy in our application. The certificate verification process lies beyond the scope of this book. Therefore, the function simply always returns the `true` constant, meaning that the certificate verification succeeded without performing the actual verification.

The three public methods comprise the interface of the `SyncSSLClient` class. The method named `connect()` performs two operations. Firstly, the TCP socket is connected to the server. The socket underlying the SSL stream is returned by the method of the SSL stream object `lowest_layer()`. Then, the `connect()` method is called on the socket with `m_ep` being passed as an argument designating the endpoint to be connected to:

```
// Connect the TCP socket.
m_ssl_stream.lowest_layer().connect(m_ep);
```

After the TCP connection is established, the `handshake()` method is called on the SSL stream object, which leads to the initiation of the handshake process. This method is synchronous and does not return until the handshake completes or an error occurs:

```
// Perform the SSL handshake.
m_ssl_stream.handshake(asio::ssl::stream_base::client);
```

After the `handshake()` method returns, both TCP and SSL (or TLS, depending on which protocol was agreed upon during the handshake process) connections are established and the effective communication can be performed.

The `close()` method shuts down the SSL connection by calling the `shutdown()` method on the SSL stream object. The `shutdown()` method is synchronous and blocks until the SSL connection is shut down or an error occurs. After this method returns, the corresponding SSL stream object cannot be used to transmit the data anymore.

The third interface method is `emulate_long_computation_op(unsigned int duration_sec)`. This method is where the I/O operations are performed. It begins with preparing the request string according to the application layer protocol. Then, the request is passed to the class' `send_request(const std::string& request)` private method, which sends it to the server. When the request is sent and the `send_request()` method returns, the `receive_response()` method is called to receive the response from the server. When the response is received, the `receive_response()` method returns the string containing the response. After this, the `emulate_long_computation_op()` method returns the response message to its caller.

Note that the `emulate_long_computation_op()`, `send_request()`, and `receive_response()` methods are almost identical to the corresponding methods defined in the `SyncTCPClient` class, which is a part of the synchronous TCP client application demonstrated in *Chapter 3, Implementing Client Applications*, which we used as a base for `SyncSSLClient` class. The only difference is that in `SyncSSLClient`, an *SSL stream object* is passed to the corresponding Boost.Asio I/O functions, while in the `SyncTCPClient` class, a *socket object* is passed to those functions. Other aspects of the mentioned methods are identical.

The main() entry point function

This function acts as a user of the `SyncSSLClient` class. Having obtained the server IP address and protocol port number, it instantiates and uses the object of the `SyncSSLClient` class to authenticate and securely communicate with the server in order to consume its service, namely, to emulate an operation on the server by performing dummy calculations for 10 seconds. The code of this function is simple and self-explanatory; thus, requires no additional comments.

See also

> ▸ The *Implementing a synchronous TCP client* recipe from *Chapter 3, Implementing Client Applications*, provides more information on how to implement a synchronous TCP client used as a base for this recipe.

Adding SSL/TLS support to server applications

SSL/TLS protocol support is usually added to the server application when the services it provides assumes transmission of sensitive data such as passwords, credit card numbers, personal data, and so on, by the client to the server. In this case, adding SSL/TLS protocol support to the server allows clients to authenticate the server and establish a secure channel to make sure that the sensitive data is protected while being transmitted.

Sometimes, a server application may want to use SSL/TLS protocol to authenticate the client; however, this is rarely the case and usually other methods are used to ensure the authenticity of the client (for example, username and password are specified when logging into a mail server).

This recipe demonstrates how to implement a synchronous iterative TCP server application supporting SSL/TLS protocol using the Boost.Asio and OpenSSL libraries. The synchronous iterative TCP server application demonstrated in the recipe named *Implementing a synchronous iterative TCP server* from *Chapter 4, Implementing Server Applications*, is taken as a base for this recipe and some code changes and additions are made to it in order to add support for SSL/TLS protocol. The code that differs from that of the base implementation of the synchronous iterative TCP server is *highlighted* so that the code directly related to SSL/TLS support is better distinguished from the rest of the code.

Getting ready...

Before setting out to this recipe, OpenSSL library must be installed and the project must be linked against it. Procedures related to the installation of the library or linking the project against it are beyond the scope of this book. Refer to the official OpenSSL documentation for more information.

Besides, because this recipe is based on another recipe named *Implementing a synchronous iterative TCP server*, from *Chapter 4, Implementing Server Applications*, it is highly advised to get acquainted with it before proceeding to this one.

How to do it...

The following code sample demonstrates the possible implementation of a synchronous TCP server application supporting SSL/TLS protocol to allow client applications to authenticate the server and protect the data being transmitted.

We begin our application by including Boost.Asio library headers and headers of some components of standard C++ libraries that we will need to implement in our application:

```
#include <boost/asio.hpp>
#include <boost/asio/ssl.hpp>

#include <thread>
#include <atomic>
#include <iostream>

using namespace boost;
```

The `<boost/asio/ssl.hpp>` header contains types and functions providing integration with OpenSSL library.

Next, we define a class responsible for handling a single client by reading the request message, processing it, and then sending back the response message. This class represents a single service provided by the server application and is named correspondingly—Service:

```cpp
class Service {
public:
  Service(){}

  void handle_client(
  asio::ssl::stream<asio::ip::tcp::socket>& ssl_stream)
  {
    try {
      // Blocks until the handshake completes.
      ssl_stream.handshake(
        asio::ssl::stream_base::server);

      asio::streambuf request;
      asio::read_until(ssl_stream, request, '\n');

      // Emulate request processing.
      int i = 0;
      while (i != 1000000)
        i++;
      std::this_thread::sleep_for(
        std::chrono::milliseconds(500));

      // Sending response.
      std::string response = "Response\n";
      asio::write(ssl_stream, asio::buffer(response));
    }
    catch (system::system_error &e) {
      std::cout << "Error occured! Error code = "
        << e.code() << ". Message: "
        << e.what();
    }
  }
};
```

Next, we define another class that represents a high-level *acceptor* concept (as compared to the low-level acceptor represented by the `asio::ip::tcp::acceptor` class). This class is responsible for accepting connection requests arriving from clients and instantiating objects of the `Service` class, which will provide the service to connected clients. This class is called Acceptor:

```cpp
class Acceptor {
public:
  Acceptor(asio::io_service& ios, unsigned short port_num) :
    m_ios(ios),
    m_acceptor(m_ios,
    asio::ip::tcp::endpoint(
    asio::ip::address_v4::any(),
    port_num)),
    m_ssl_context(asio::ssl::context::sslv23_server)
  {
    // Setting up the context.
    m_ssl_context.set_options(
      boost::asio::ssl::context::default_workarounds
      | boost::asio::ssl::context::no_sslv2
      | boost::asio::ssl::context::single_dh_use);

    m_ssl_context.set_password_callback(
      [this](std::size_t max_length,
      asio::ssl::context::password_purpose purpose)
      -> std::string
        {return get_password(max_length, purpose);}
    );

    m_ssl_context.use_certificate_chain_file("server.crt");
    m_ssl_context.use_private_key_file("server.key",
      boost::asio::ssl::context::pem);
    m_ssl_context.use_tmp_dh_file("dhparams.pem");

    // Start listening for incoming connection requests.
    m_acceptor.listen();
  }

  void accept() {
    asio::ssl::stream<asio::ip::tcp::socket>
    ssl_stream(m_ios, m_ssl_context);
```

```
    m_acceptor.accept(ssl_stream.lowest_layer());

    Service svc;
    svc.handle_client(ssl_stream);
  }

private:
  std::string get_password(std::size_t max_length,
    asio::ssl::context::password_purpose purpose) const
  {
    return "pass";
  }

private:
  asio::io_service& m_ios;
  asio::ip::tcp::acceptor m_acceptor;

  asio::ssl::context m_ssl_context;
};
```

Now we define a class that represents the server itself. The class is named correspondingly—Server:

```
class Server {
public:
  Server() : m_stop(false) {}

  void start(unsigned short port_num) {
    m_thread.reset(new std::thread([this, port_num]() {
      run(port_num);
    }));
  }

  void stop() {
    m_stop.store(true);
    m_thread->join();
  }

private:
  void run(unsigned short port_num) {
    Acceptor acc(m_ios, port_num);

    while (!m_stop.load()) {
      acc.accept();
    }
```

```
    }

    std::unique_ptr<std::thread> m_thread;
    std::atomic<bool> m_stop;
    asio::io_service m_ios;
};
```

Eventually, we implement the `main()` application entry point function that demonstrates how to use the `Server` class. This function is identical to the one defined in the recipe from *Chapter 4, Implementing Server Applications*, that we took as a base for this recipe:

```
int main()
{
  unsigned short port_num = 3333;

  try {
    Server srv;
    srv.start(port_num);

    std::this_thread::sleep_for(std::chrono::seconds(60));

    srv.stop();
  }
  catch (system::system_error &e) {
    std::cout    << "Error occured! Error code = "
    << e.code() << ". Message: "
        << e.what();
  }

  return 0;
}
```

Note that the last two components of the server application, namely, the `Server` class and the `main()` application entry point function are identical to the corresponding components defined in the recipe from *Chapter 4, Implementing Server Applications*, that we took as a base for this recipe.

How it works...

The sample server application consists of four components: the `Service`, `Acceptor`, and `Server` classes and the `main()`, application entry point function, which demonstrates how to use the `Server` class. Because the source code and the purpose of the `Server` class and the `main()` entry point function are identical to those of the corresponding components defined in the recipe from *Chapter 4, Implementing Server Applications*, that we took as a base for this recipe, we will not discuss them here. We will only consider the `Service` and `Acceptor` classes that were updated to provide support for SSL/TLS protocol.

The Service class

The `Service` class is the key functional component in the application. While other components are infrastructural in their purpose, this class implements the actual function (or service) required by the clients.

The `Service` class is quite simple and consists of a single method `handle_client()`. As its input argument, this method accepts a reference to an object representing an SSL stream that wraps a TCP socket connected to a particular client.

The method begins with performing an SSL/TLS **handshake** by invoking the `handshake()` method on the `ssl_stream` object. This method is synchronous and does not return until the handshake completes or an error occurs.

After the handshake has completed, a request message is synchronously read from the SSL stream until a new line ASCII symbol \n is encountered. Then, the request is processed. In our sample application, request processing is trivial and dummy and consists in running a loop performing one million increment operations and then putting the thread to sleep for half a second. After this, the response message is prepared and sent back to the client.

Exceptions that may be thrown by the Boost.Asio functions and methods are caught and handled in the `handle_client()` method and are not propagated to the method's caller so that, if handling of one client fails, the server continues working.

Note that the `handle_client()` method is very similar to the corresponding method defined in the recipe *Implementing a synchronous iterative TCP server*, from *Chapter 4, Implementing Server Applications*, that we took as a base for this recipe. The difference consists in the fact that in this recipe, the `handle_client()` method operates on an object representing an SSL stream as opposed to an object representing a TCP socket being operated on in the base implementation of the method. Besides, an additional operation—an SSL/TLS handshake—is performed in the method defined in this recipe.

The Acceptor class

The `Acceptor` class is a part of the server application infrastructure. Each object of this class owns an instance of the `asio::ssl::context` class named `m_ssl_context`. This member represents an **SSL context**. Basically, the `asio::ssl::contex` class is a wrapper around the `SSL_CTX` data structure defined by OpenSSL library. Objects of this class contain global settings and parameters used by other objects and functions involved in the process of communication using SSL/TLS protocol.

The `m_ssl_context` object, when instantiated, is passed a `asio::ssl::context::sslv23_server` value to its constructor to designate that the SSL context will be used by the application playing a role of a *server* only and that multiple secure protocols should be supported, including multiple versions of SSL and TLS. This value defined by Boost.Asio corresponds to a value representing a connection method returned by the `SSLv23_server_method()` function defined by OpenSSL library.

The SSL context is configured in the `Acceptor` class' constructor. The context options, password callback and files containing digital certificates, and private keys and Diffie-Hellman protocol parameters, are specified there.

After SSL context has been configured, the `listen()` method is called on the acceptor object in the `Acceptor` class' constructor to start listening for connection requests from the clients.

The `Acceptor` class exposes a single `accept()` public method. This method, when called, first instantiates an object of the `asio::ssl::stream<asio::ip::tcp::socket>` class named `ssl_stream`, representing an SSL/TLS communication channel with the underlying TCP socket. Then, the `accept()` method is called on the `m_acceptor` acceptor object to accept a connection. The TCP socket object owned by `ssl_stream`, returned by its `lowest_layer()` method, is passed to the `accept()` method as an input argument. When a new connection is established, an instance of the `Service` class is created and its `handle_client()` method is called, which performs communication with the client and request handling.

See also

> ▸ The *Implementing synchronous iterative TCP server* recipe from *Chapter 4, Implementing Server Applications*, provides more information on how to implement a synchronous TCP server used as a base for this recipe.

6

Other Topics

In this chapter, we will cover the following recipes:

- ▶ Using composite buffers for scatter/gather operations
- ▶ Using timers
- ▶ Getting and setting socket options
- ▶ Performing a stream-based I/O

Introduction

This final chapter includes four recipes that stand somewhat apart from those in previous chapters that demonstrate the core Boost.Asio concepts, covering the majority of typical use cases. However, it does not mean that recipes demonstrated in this chapter are less important. On the contrary, they are very important and even critical to specific cases. However, they will be required less often in typical distributed applications.

Though most applications will not require scatter/gather I/O operations and composite buffers, for some, which keep different parts of messages in separate buffers, such facilities may turn out to be very usable and convenient.

The Boost.Asio timer is a powerful instrument that allows measuring time intervals. Often, this is used to set deadlines for the operations that may last unpredictably long and to interrupt those operations if they do not complete after running for a certain period of time. For many distributed applications, such an instrument is critical, taking into account the fact that Boost. Asio does not provide a way to specify a timeout for potentially long-running operations. In addition to this, timers provided by Boost.Asio can be used to solve other tasks that are not related to network communication.

Tools that allow getting and setting socket options are quite important as well. When developing a simple network application, the developer may be fully satisfied with the socket equipped with default values of the options that are automatically set during instantiation of the socket object. However, in more sophisticated cases, it may be absolutely necessary to reconfigure the socket by customizing the values of its options.

Boost.Asio classes that wrap the socket and provide a stream-like interface to it allow us to create simple and elegant distributed applications. And simplicity is known to be one of the key characteristics of a good software.

Now, let's move on to a detailed consideration of the mentioned topics.

Using composite buffers for scatter/gather operations

The *Using fixed-length I/O buffers* recipe in *Chapter 2, I/O Operations*, introduces simple I/O buffers, but only slightly touches upon scatter/gather operations and composite buffers. In this recipe, we are going to consider this topic in more detail.

A composite buffer is basically a complex buffer that consists of two or more simple buffers (contiguous blocks of memory) distributed over the process' address space. Such buffers become especially handy in two situations.

The first situation is when the application needs a buffer either to store the message before sending it to the remote application or to receive the message sent by the remote application. The problem is that the size of the message is so big that allocating a single contiguous buffer that is sufficient to store it may fail due to the process' address space fragmentation. In this case, allocating multiple smaller buffers, whose sizes when summed would be enough to store the data, and combining them in a single composite buffer is a good solution to the problem.

Another situation is actually the first one inverted. Due to specificity of the design of the application, the message to be sent to the remote application is broken into several parts and stored in different buffers, or if the message to be received from the remote application needs to be broken into several parts, each of which should be stored in a separate buffer for further processing. In both the cases, combining several buffers into one composite buffer and then using scatter send or gather receive operations would be a good approach to the problem.

In this recipe, we will see how to create composite buffers and use them in scatter/gather I/O operations.

Getting ready...

To understand the content presented in this recipe, it is desirable to be familiar with the content of the *Using fixed-length I/O buffers* recipe in *Chapter 2, I/O Operations*, that provides a general overview of Boost.Asio's fixed length I/O buffers. Therefore, it is recommended to get acquainted with the *Using fixed-length I/O buffers* recipe before proceeding with this one.

How to do it...

Let's consider two algorithms and corresponding code samples that describe how to create and prepare a composite buffer that is to be used with Boost.Asio I/O operations. The first algorithm deals with the composite buffer intended for use in gather output operations and the second one for scatter input operations.

Preparing a composite buffer for gather output operations

The following is the algorithm and corresponding code sample that describe how to prepare the composite buffer that is to be used with the socket's method that performs output operations such as `asio::ip::tcp::socket::send()` or a free function such as `asio::write()`:

1. Allocate as many memory buffers as needed to perform the task at hand. Note that this step does not involve any functionality or data types from Boost.Asio.

2. Fill the buffers with data to be output.

3. Create an instance of a class that satisfies the `ConstBufferSequence` or `MultipleBufferSequence` concept's requirements, representing a composite buffer.

4. Add simple buffers to the composite buffer. Each simple buffer should be represented as an instance of the `asio::const_buffer` or `asio::mutable_buffer` classes.

5. The composite buffer is ready to be used with Boost.Asio output functions.

Let's say we want to send a string `Hello my friend!` to the remote application, but our message was broken into three parts and each part was stored in a separate buffer. What we can do is represent our three buffers as a composite buffer, and then, use it in the output operation. This is how we will do it in the following code:

```
#include <boost/asio.hpp>

using namespace boost;

int main()
{
  // Steps 1 and 2. Create and fill simple buffers.
  const char* part1 = "Hello ";
```

```
const char* part2 = "my ";
const char* part3 = "friend!";

// Step 3. Create an object representing a composite buffer.
std::vector<asio::const_buffer> composite_buffer;

// Step 4. Add simple buffers to the composite buffer.
composite_buffer.push_back(asio::const_buffer(part1, 6));
composite_buffer.push_back(asio::const_buffer(part2, 3));
composite_buffer.push_back(asio::const_buffer(part3, 7));

// Step 5. Now composite_buffer can be used with Boost.Asio
// output operations as if it was a simple buffer represented
// by contiguous block of memory.

return 0;
}
```

Preparing a composite buffer for an input operation

The following is the algorithm and corresponding code sample that describe how to prepare the composite buffer that is to be used with the `socket`'s method that performs an input operation such as `asio::ip::tcp::socket::receive()` or a free function such as `asio::read()`:

1. Allocate as many memory buffers as required to perform the task at hand. The sum of the sizes of the buffers must be equal to or greater than the size of the expected message to be received in these buffers. Note that this step does not involve any functionalities or data types from Boost.Asio.

2. Create an instance of a class that satisfies the `MutableBufferSequence` concept's requirements that represents a composite buffer.

3. Add simple buffers to the composite buffer. Each simple buffer should be represented as an instance of the `asio::mutable_buffer` class.

4. The composite buffer is ready to be used with Boost.Asio input operations.

Let's imagine a hypothetical situation, where we want to receive 16 bytes long messages from the server. However, we do not have a buffer that can fit the entire message. Instead, we have three buffers: 6, 3, and 7 bytes long. To create a buffer in which we can receive 16 bytes of data, we can join our three small buffers into a composite one. This is how we do it in the following code:

```
#include <boost/asio.hpp>

using namespace boost;
```

```
int main()
{
    // Step 1. Allocate simple buffers.
    char part1[6];
    char part2[3];
    char part3[7];

    // Step 2. Create an object representing a composite buffer.
    std::vector<asio::mutable_buffer> composite_buffer;

    // Step 3. Add simple buffers to the composite buffer object.
    composite_buffer.push_back(asio::mutable_buffer(part1,
    sizeof(part1)));
    composite_buffer.push_back(asio::mutable_buffer(part2,
    sizeof(part2)));
    composite_buffer.push_back(asio::mutable_buffer(part3,
    sizeof(part3)));

    // Now composite_buffer can be used with Boost.Asio
    // input operation as if it was a simple buffer
    // represented by contiguous block of memory.

    return 0;
}
```

How it works...

Let's see how the first sample works. It starts with allocating three read-only buffers that are filled with parts of the message string `Hello my friend!`.

In the next step, an instance of the `std::vector<asio::const_buffer>` class is created, which is the embodiment of the composite buffer. The instance is given the corresponding name, `composite_buffer`. Because the `std::vector<asio::const_buffer>` class satisfies the requirements of `ConstBufferSequence`, its objects can be used as composite buffers and can be passed to Boost.Asio gather output functions and methods as arguments that represent the data source.

In step 4, each of our three buffers is represented as an instance of the `asio::const_buffer` class and added to the composite buffer. Because all Boost.Asio output functions and methods that work with fixed-sized buffers are designed to work with composite buffers as well, our `composite_buffer` object can be used with them like a simple buffer.

The second sample works quite similar to the first one. The only difference is that because the composite buffer created in this sample is intended to be used as a data destination (rather than a data source as it is in the first sample), the three simple buffers added to it are created as writable ones and are represented as instances of the `asio::mutable_buffer` class when added to the composite buffer.

Another thing to note about the second sample is that because the composite buffer created in this sample is composed of mutable buffers, it can be used in both gather output and scatter input operations. In this particular sample, the initial buffers (`part1`, `part2`, and `part3`) are not filled with any data and they contain garbage; and therefore, using them in output operations is senseless unless they are filled with meaningful data.

See also

- The *Using fixed-length I/O buffers* recipe in *Chapter 2, I/O Operations*, provides more information on fixed size simple buffers
- The *Using extensible stream-oriented I/O buffers* recipe in *Chapter 2, I/O Operations*, demonstrates how to use classes provided by Boost.Asio, representing different types of buffers—extensible buffers

Using timers

Timing is a very important aspect of software systems in general and distributed applications in particular. Therefore a hardware timer—a device used to measure time intervals—is essential component of any computer and all modern operating systems provide interface allowing applications to use it.

There are two typical use cases related to the timer. The first one assumes that the application wants to know the current time and asks the operating system to find it out. The second use case is when the application asks the operating system to notify it (usually, by means of invoking a callback) when a certain amount of time elapses.

The second use case is particularly important when it comes to developing distributed applications with Boost.Asio because a timer is the only way to implement the timeout mechanism for asynchronous operations.

The Boost.Asio library includes several classes that implement timers, which we will consider in this recipe.

How to do it...

The Boost.Asio library provides two template classes that implement timers. One of them is `asio::basic_deadline_timer<>`, which was the only one available before Boost.Asio 1.49 version was released. In version 1.49, the second timer `asio::basic_waitable_timer<>` class template was introduced.

The `asio::basic_deadline_timer<>` class template was designed to be compatible with the Boost.Chrono library and internally relies on the functionality it provides. This template class is somewhat outdated and provides a limited functionality. Therefore, we will not consider it in this recipe.

On the contrary, a newer `asio::basic_waitable_timer<>` class template, which is compatible with the C++11 `chrono` library is more flexible and provides more functionalities. Boost.Asio includes three `typedefs` for classes that are generically derived from the `asio::basic_waitable_timer<>` template class:

```
typedef basic_waitable_timer< std::chrono::system_clock >
    system_timer;
typedef basic_waitable_timer< std::chrono::steady_clock >
    steady_timer;
typedef basic_waitable_timer< std::chrono::high_resolution_clock >
    high_resolution_timer;
```

The `asio::system_timer` class is based on the `std::chrono::system_clock` class, which represents a system-wide real-time clock. This clock (and so is the timer) is influenced by external changes of the current system time. Therefore, the `asio::system_timer` class is a good choice when we need to set up a timer that will notify us when a certain absolute time point is reached (for instance, 13h:15m:45s), taking into account the system clock shifts made after the timer was set up. However, this timer is not good at measuring time intervals (for instance, 35 seconds from now) because the system clock shifts may result in the timer expiring sooner or later than the actual interval elapses.

The `asio::steady_timer` class is based on the `std::chrono::steady_clock` class, which represents a steady clock that is not influenced by the system clock changes. It means that `asio::steady_timer` is a good choice to measure intervals.

The last timer `asio::high_resolution_timer` class is based on the `std::chrono::high_resolution_clock` class, which represents a high-resolution system clock. It can be used in cases when high precision in time measurement is required.

In distributed applications implemented with the Boost.Asio library, timers are usually used to implement timeout periods for asynchronous operations. Just after the asynchronous operation starts (for example, `asio::async_read()`), the application will start a timer set up to expire after a certain period of time, *a timeout period*. When the timer expires, the application checks whether the asynchronous operation has completed and if it has not, the operation is considered timed out and is canceled.

Because a steady timer is not influenced by the system clock shifts, it is the best fit to implement the timeout mechanism.

 Note that on some platforms, steady clocks are not available and the corresponding class that represents a std::chrono::steady_clock exhibits behavior that is identical to that of std::chrono::stystem_clock, which means that just like the latter, it is influenced by the changes of the system clock. It is advised to refer to the documentation of the platform and corresponding C++ standard library implementation to find out whether the steady clock is actually *steady*.

Let's consider a somewhat unrealistic but representative sample application that demonstrates how to create, start, and cancel Boost.Asio timers. In our sample, we will create and start two steady timers one by one. When the first timer expires, we will cancel the second one, before it has a chance to expire.

We begin our sample application with including the necessary Boost.Asio headers and the using directive:

```
#include <boost/asio/steady_timer.hpp>
#include <iostream>

using namespace boost;
```

Next, we define the only component in our application: the main() entry point function:

```
int main()
{
```

Like almost any nontrivial Boost.Asio application, we need an instance of the asio::io_service class:

```
    asio::io_service ios;
```

Then, we create and start the first t1 timer, which is set up to expire in 2 seconds:

```
    asio::steady_timer t1(ios);
    t1.expires_from_now(std::chrono::seconds(2));
```

Then, we create and start the second t2 timer, which is set up to expire in 5 seconds. It should definitely expire later than the first timer:

```
    asio::steady_timer t2(ios);
    t2.expires_from_now(std::chrono::seconds(5));
```

Now, we define and set a callback function that is to be called when the first timer expires:

```
t1.async_wait([&t2](boost::system::error_code ec) {
    if (ec == 0) {
        std::cout << "Timer #2 has expired!" << std::endl;
    }
    else if (ec == asio::error::operation_aborted) {
        std::cout << "Timer #2 has been cancelled!"
                    << std::endl;
    }
    else {
        std::cout << "Error occured! Error code = "
            << ec.value()
            << ". Message: " << ec.message()
                    << std::endl;
    }

    t2.cancel();
});
```

Then, we define and set another callback function that is to be called when the second timer expires:

```
t2.async_wait([](boost::system::error_code ec) {
    if (ec == 0) {
        std::cout << "Timer #2 has expired!" << std::endl;
    }
    else if (ec == asio::error::operation_aborted) {
        std::cout << "Timer #2 has been cancelled!"
    << std::endl;
    }
    else {
        std::cout << "Error occured! Error code = "
            << ec.value()
            << ". Message: " << ec.message()
    << std::endl;
    }
});
```

In the last step, we call the `run()` method on the instance of the `asio::io_service` class:

```
ios.run();

    return 0;
}
```

Now, our sample application is ready.

How it works...

Now, let's track the application's execution path to better understand how it works.

The `main()` function begins with creating an instance of the `asio::io_service` class. We need it because just like sockets, acceptors, resolvers, and other components defined by the Boost.Asio library, which use operating system services, timers require an instance of the `asio::io_service` class as well.

In the next step, the first timer named `t1` is instantiated and then the `expires_from_now()` method is called on it. This method switches the timer to a non-expired state and starts it. It accepts an argument that represents the duration of the time interval, after which the timer should expire. In our sample, we pass an argument that represents the duration of 2 seconds, which means that in 2 seconds, from the moment when the timer starts, it will expire and all those who are waiting for this timer's expiration event will be notified.

Next, the second timer named `t2` is created, which is then started and set up to expire in 5 seconds.

When both the timers are started, we asynchronously wait for the timers' expiration events. In other words, we register callbacks on each of the two timers, which will be invoked when the corresponding timers expire. To do this, we call the timer's `async_wait()` method and pass the pointer to the callback function as an argument. The `async_wait()` method expects its argument to be a pointer to the function that has the following signature:

```
void callback(
    const boost::system::error_code& ec);
```

The callback function accepts a single `ec` argument, which designates the wait completion status. In our sample application, we use lambda functions as expiration callbacks for both the timers.

When both timer expiration callbacks are set, the `run()` method is called on the `ios` object. The method blocks until both the timers expire. The thread, in the context of which the method `run()` is invoked, will be used to invoke the expiration callbacks.

When the first timer expires, the corresponding callback function is invoked. It checks the wait completion status and outputs corresponding messages to the standard output stream. And then it cancels the second timer by calling the `cancel()` method on the `t2` object.

The canceling of the second timer leads to the expiration callback being called with the status code, notifying that the timer was canceled before expiration. The expiration callback of the second timer checks the expiration status and outputs corresponding messages to the standard output stream and returns.

When both callbacks are completed, the `run()` method returns and the execution of the `main()` function runs to the end. This is when the execution of the application is completed.

Getting and setting socket options

The socket's properties and its behavior can be configured by changing the values of its various options. When the socket object is instantiated, its options have default values. In many cases, the socket configured by default is a perfect fit, whereas in others, it may be needed to fine tune the socket by changing values of its options so that it meets the requirements of the application.

In this recipe, we will see how to get and set socket options with Boost.Asio.

Getting ready...

This recipe assumes familiarity with the content provided in *Chapter 1, The Basics*.

How to do it...

Each socket option, whose value can be set or obtained by means of a functionality provided by Boost.Asio, is represented by a separate class. The complete list of classes that represent setting or getting socket options, which are supported by Boost.Asio, can be found on this Boost.Asio documentation page at `http://www.boost.org/doc/libs/1_58_0/doc/html/boost_asio/reference/socket_base.html`.

Note that there are fewer classes that represent socket options listed on this page than the options that can be set or obtained from a native socket (an object of the underlying operating system). This is because Boost.Asio supports only a limited amount of socket options. To set or obtain values of other socket options, developers may need to extend the Boost.Asio library by adding classes that represent the required options. However, the topic on the extension of the Boost.Asio library is beyond the scope of this book. We will focus on how to work with socket options that are supported by the library out of the box.

Let's consider a hypothetical situation where we want to make the size of the socket's receive buffer two times bigger than whatever its size is now. To do this, we first need to get the current size of the buffer, then multiply it by two, and finally, set the value obtained after multiplication as the new receive buffer size.

The following sample demonstrates how to do this in the following code:

```cpp
#include <boost/asio.hpp>
#include <iostream>

using namespace boost;

int main()
{
  try {
    asio::io_service ios;

    // Create and open a TCP socket.
    asio::ip::tcp::socket sock(ios, asio::ip::tcp::v4());

    // Create an object representing receive buffer
    //  size option.
    asio::socket_base::receive_buffer_size cur_buf_size;

    // Get the currently set value of the option.
    sock.get_option(cur_buf_size);

    std::cout << "Current receive buffer size is "
      << cur_buf_size.value() << " bytes."
      << std::endl;

    // Create an object representing receive buffer
    //  size option with new value.
    asio::socket_base::receive_buffer_size
      new_buf_size(cur_buf_size.value() * 2);

    // Set new value of the option.
    sock.set_option(new_buf_size);

    std::cout << "New receive buffer size is "
      << new_buf_size.value() << " bytes."
      << std::endl;
  }
  catch (system::system_error &e) {
    std::cout << "Error occured! Error code = " << e.code()
      << ". Message: " << e.what();

    return e.code().value();
  }

  return 0;
}
```

How it works...

Our sample consists of a single component: the `main()` entry point function. This function begins with creating an instance of the `asio::io_service` class. This instance is then used to create an object that represents a TCP socket.

Note the usage of the socket class constructor, which creates and *opens* the socket. Before we can get or set options on a particular socket object, the corresponding socket must be opened. This is because before the Boost.Asio socket object is opened, the underlying native *socket* object of the corresponding operating system is not yet allocated, and there is nothing to set the options on or get them from.

Next, an instance of the `asio::socket_base::receive_buffer_size` class is instantiated. This class represents an option that controls the size of the socket's receive buffer. To obtain the current value of the option, the `get_option()` method is called on the socket object and the reference to the option object is passed to it as an argument.

The `get_option()` method deduces the option that is requested by the type of the argument passed to it. Then, it stores the corresponding option's value in the option object and returns. The value of the option can be obtained from the object that represents the corresponding option by invoking the object's `value()` method, which returns the value of the option.

After the current value of receive buffer size option is obtained and output to the standard output stream, in order to set the new value of this option, the `main()` function proceeds with creating one more instance of the `asio::socket_base::receive_buffer_size` class named `new_buf_size`. This instance represents the same option as the first instance, `cur_buf_size`, but this one contains the new value. The new option value is passed to the option object as an argument of its constructor.

After the option object that contains the new receive buffer size option value is constructed, the reference to it is passed as an argument to the socket's `set_option()` method. Like `get_option()`, this method deduces the option to be set by the type of the argument passed to it, and then, sets the corresponding option value, making the new value equal to the one stored in the option object.

In the last step, the new option's value is output to the standard output stream.

Performing a stream-based I/O

The concepts of a stream and stream-based I/O are powerful in their expressiveness and elegance when used properly. Sometimes, most of the application's source code consists of stream-based I/O operations. The source code readability and maintainability of such an application would be increased if network communication modules were implemented by means of stream-based operations as well.

Fortunately, Boost.Asio provides tools that allow us to implement inter-process communication in a stream-based fashion. In this recipe, we will see how to use them.

How to do it...

The Boost.Asio library contains the `asio::ip::tcp::iostream` wrapper class that provides an I/O stream-like interface to the TCP socket objects, which allows us to express inter-process communication operations in terms of stream-based operations.

Let's consider a TCP client application, which takes advantage of a stream-based I/O provided by Boost.Asio. When using this approach, the TCP client application becomes as simple as the following code:

```cpp
#include <boost/asio.hpp>
#include <iostream>

using namespace boost;

int main()
{
  asio::ip::tcp::iostream stream("localhost", "3333");
  if (!stream) {
    std::cout << "Error occurred! Error code = "
      << stream.error().value()
      << ". Message = " << stream.error().message()
      << std::endl;

    return -1;
  }

  stream << "Request.";
  stream.flush();

  std::cout << "Response: " << stream.rdbuf();

  return 0;
}
```

How it works...

The sample TCP client is quite simple and consists of a single component: the `main()` entry point function. The `main()` function begins with creating an instance of the `asio::ip::tcp::iostream` class, which wraps a TCP socket and provides an I/O stream-like interface to it.

The `stream` object is constructed with a constructor that accepts a server DNS name and a protocol port number and automatically tries to resolve the DNS name and then tries to connect to that server. Note that the port number is represented as a string rather than an integer. This is because both arguments passed to this constructor are directly used to create the resolver query, which requires the port number to be represented as a string (it should be expressed as a service name such as `http`, `ftp`, and so on or a port number that is represented as a string such as "80", "8081", "3333", and so on).

Alternatively, we can construct the `stream` object using the default constructor, which does not perform the DNS name resolution and connection. Then, when the object is constructed, we can call the `connect()` method on it by specifying the DNS name and protocol port number in order to perform the resolution and connect the socket.

Next, the state of the stream object is tested to find out whether the connection has succeeded. And if the stream object is in a bad or erroneous state, the appropriate message is output to the standard output stream and the application exits. The `error()` method of the `asio::ip::tcp::iostream` class returns an instance of the `boost::system::error_code` class, which provides the information about the last error that occurred in the stream.

However, if the stream has been successfully connected to the server, the output operation is performed on it, which sends the string `Request`, to the server. After this, the `flush()` method is called on the stream object to make sure that all the buffered data is pushed to the server.

In the last step, the input operation is performed on the stream to read all the data that was received from the server as a response. The received message is output to the standard output stream. After this, the `main()` function returns and the application exits.

There's more...

Not only can we implement the client-side I/O in a stream-oriented fashion using the `asio::ip::tcp::iostream` class, we can also perform I/O operations on the server side as well. In addition to this, this class allows us to specify timeouts for operations, which makes a stream-based I/O more advantageous than a normal synchronous I/O. Let's take a look at how this is done.

Implementing a server-side I/O

The following code snippet demonstrates how to implement a simple server that performs a stream-based I/O using the `asio::ip::tcp::iostream` class:

```
// ...
asio::io_service io_service;

asio::ip::tcp::acceptor acceptor(io_service,
```

```
        asio::ip::tcp::endpoint(asio::ip::tcp::v4(), 3333));

    asio::ip::tcp::iostream stream;

  acceptor.accept(*stream.rdbuf());
  std::cout << "Request: " << stream.rdbuf();
  stream << "Response.";
  // ...
```

This code snippet demonstrates a piece of source code of a simple server application. It creates instances of acceptors and the `asio::ip::tcp::iostream` classes. And then, the interesting thing happens.

The `accept()` method is invoked on the `acceptor` object. As an argument, this method is passed an object, a pointer to which is returned by the `rdbuf()` method called on the `stream` object. The `rdbuf()` method of the `stream` object returns a pointer to the stream buffer object. This stream buffer object is an instance of a class, which is inherited from the `asio::ip::tcp::socket` class, which means that the stream buffer used by objects of the `asio::ip::tcp ::iostream` class plays two roles: one of a stream buffer and another of a socket. Therefore, this `twofold` stream buffer/socket object can be used as a normal active socket to connect and communicate with the client application.

When the connection request is accepted and the connection is established, further communication with the client is done in a stream-fashioned style just like it is done in the client application, as demonstrated earlier in this recipe.

Setting timeout intervals

Because I/O operations are provided by the `asio::ip::tcp::stream` class block the thread of execution, and they potentially may run for a substantial amount of time, the class provides a way to set a timeout period that, when it runs out, leads to the interruption of the operation that currently blocks the thread, if any.

The timeout interval can be set by the `expires_from_now()` method of the `asio::ip::tcp::stream` class. This method accepts the duration of the timeout interval as an input parameter and starts the internal timer. If at the moment, when the timer expires, an I/O operation is still in progress, that operation is considered timed out and is, therefore, forcefully interrupted.

Index

Thank you for buying
Boost.Asio C++ Network Programming Cookbook

About Packt Publishing

Packt, pronounced 'packed', published its first book, *Mastering phpMyAdmin for Effective MySQL Management*, in April 2004, and subsequently continued to specialize in publishing highly focused books on specific technologies and solutions.

Our books and publications share the experiences of your fellow IT professionals in adapting and customizing today's systems, applications, and frameworks. Our solution-based books give you the knowledge and power to customize the software and technologies you're using to get the job done. Packt books are more specific and less general than the IT books you have seen in the past. Our unique business model allows us to bring you more focused information, giving you more of what you need to know, and less of what you don't.

Packt is a modern yet unique publishing company that focuses on producing quality, cutting-edge books for communities of developers, administrators, and newbies alike. For more information, please visit our website at www.packtpub.com.

About Packt Open Source

In 2010, Packt launched two new brands, Packt Open Source and Packt Enterprise, in order to continue its focus on specialization. This book is part of the Packt open source brand, home to books published on software built around open source licenses, and offering information to anybody from advanced developers to budding web designers. The Open Source brand also runs Packt's open source Royalty Scheme, by which Packt gives a royalty to each open source project about whose software a book is sold.

Writing for Packt

We welcome all inquiries from people who are interested in authoring. Book proposals should be sent to author@packtpub.com. If your book idea is still at an early stage and you would like to discuss it first before writing a formal book proposal, then please contact us; one of our commissioning editors will get in touch with you.

We're not just looking for published authors; if you have strong technical skills but no writing experience, our experienced editors can help you develop a writing career, or simply get some additional reward for your expertise.

Learning Boost C++ Libraries

ISBN: 978-1-78355-121-7   Paperback: 558 pages

Solve practical programming problems using powerful, portable, and expressive libraries from Boost

1. Learn to apply the breadth of Boost libraries, including containers, smart pointers, regular expressions, threads, network I/O, and other utilities through practical programming examples.

2. Write clear and succinct C++ code that is efficient and maintainable.

3. Speed up using the Boost libraries without any prior knowledge, using an in-depth tutorial introduction.

Boost C++ Application Development Cookbook

ISBN: 978-1-84951-488-0   Paperback: 348 pages

Over 80 practical, task-based recipes to create applications using Boost libraries

1. Explores how to write a program once and then use it on Linux, Windows, MacOS, and Android operating systems.

2. Includes everyday use recipes for multithreading, networking, metaprogramming, and generic programming from a Boost library developer.

3. Take advantage of the real power of Boost and C++ to get a good grounding in using it in any project.

Please check **www.PacktPub.com** for information on our titles

Learning Object-Oriented Programming

ISBN: 978-1-78528-963-7   Paperback: 280 pages

Explore and crack the OOP code in Python, JavaScript, and C#

1. Write reusable code that defines and makes objects interact with one another.

2. Discover the differences in inheritance and polymorphism in Python, JavaScript, and C#.

3. Capture objects from real-world elements and create object-oriented code that represents them.

Objective-C Memory Management Essentials

ISBN: 978-1-84969-712-5   Paperback: 200 pages

Learn and put into practice various memory management techniques in Objective-C to create robust · iOS applications

1. Learn about the concepts of memory management in Objective-C.

2. Get introduced to Swift, an innovative new programming language for Cocoa and Cocoa Touch.

3. A step-by-step approach to various memory management techniques with lots of sample code and Xcode projects for your reference.

Please check **www.PacktPub.com** for information on our titles

Lightning Source UK Ltd.
Milton Keynes UK
UKHW032135191118
332603UK00005B/803/P